Celebrating The Birth Of The Savior

Celebrating The Birth Of The Savior

DISCOVERING THE BLESSINGS OF ADVENT AND CHRISTMAS

C. Welton Gaddy

Nashville, Tennessee

4260-63

ISBN: 0-8054-6063-2

Dewey Decimal Classification: 263.91
Subject Heading: WORSHIP PROGRAMS // JESUS CHRIST-NATIVITY
Library of Congress Card Catalog Number: 93-20254
Printed in the United States of America.

Unless otherwise stated, all Scripture quotations
are from the *Revised Standard Version* of the Bible,
copyright © 1946, 1952, 1971, 1973.

Scripture quotations marked KJV are from the *King James Version* of the Bible.

Scripture quotations marked GNB are from the *Good News Bible,*
the Bible in Today's English Version: Old Testament, copyright ©
American Bible Society 1976; New Testament, copyright ©
American Bible Society 1966, 1971, 1976. Used by permission.

Scripture quotations marked NIV are from the Holy Bible, *New International Version,*
copyright © 1973, 1978, 1984 by International Bible Society.

Library of Congress Cataloging-in-Publication Data

Gaddy, C. Welton.
    Celebrating the birth of the Savior / C. Welton Gaddy.
      p.   cm.
    ISBN 0-8054-6063-2
    1. Advent.   2. Christmas.   I. Title.
BV40.G33   1993
263'.91—dc20
                                                93-20254
                                                  CIP

To
One man and six women
Who made up the house of seven Grabiels
James Russell Grabiel (in memoriam)
Julia Elizabeth Hawkins Grabiel
Mary Elizabeth Grabiel Hudson
Julia Mae Grabiel Gaddy
Harriette Jo Grabiel Brandon
Bette Sue Grabiel Robison
Mitzi Lou Grabiel Gates
For whom Christmas is a festival
for unwrapping joy, unleashing laughter,
and strewing gladness all around

CONTENTS

PREFACE

*C*hristmas, I have known forever. At least it seems that way. But not Advent. For many years I was not even aware of the season of Advent or its significance in relation to Christmas. *Advent*—the word means "a coming"—is the title given to the four-week period prior to Christmas. The primary purpose of the season of Advent is preparation—preparation for a Christian celebration of Christmas as the birthday of the Savior. Advent is a time for studying biblical prophecies and promises related to the Messiah, engaging in repentance, experiencing renewal, learning the spiritual discipline of waiting, and readying life for a joyful reception of Jesus.

Apart from the strong encouragement of several Southern Baptist laypeople, I might never have known the profound significance of Advent. Fortunately, in my first pastorate after seminary graduate studies, a small group of men and women approached me with the request that I lead the congregation in an observance of Advent. That initial pilgrimage through Advent exceeded my highest expectations. Since that time Advent has been an annual season of spiritual challenge, commitment, and worship for me and for the congregations in which I have ministered.

Typically, by late summer or early fall of each year, I receive several requests from church leaders interested in observing Advent in their congregations. All are seeking interpretations of the season, suggestions regarding the kinds of experiences appropriate to it, and resources for Advent-related worship. Those inquiries, which I welcome, first prompted thoughts about producing a volume like this.

On the pages that follow, there are a variety of materials related to Advent. The introduction is a brief description of the situation in which Advent is experienced—our need for Advent and our best response to it. Next, in part 1, after a confession of my initial suspicion regarding Advent, I sketch a history of the season, enumerate several of its most important traditions, and explore the potential values in Advent observances. Based upon my present conviction about the spiritual significance of Advent, I also offer several suggestions for worship activities that can be meaningful components of the season.

Parts 2 through 4 consist of three biblically based and thematically related collections of resources for use in Advent worship experiences. If one chapter is given attention during each of the four weeks of a season of Advent, these materials can be used for three different years. The final section of this volume, part 5, contains three essays to be read as a part of a celebration of Christmas.

Both individuals and groups can use these materials. Worship leaders can draw from the words on these pages as they prepare to speak their own words during this season. Discussion groups or Bible study groups can focus on one essay at a time (in parts 1 and 3) as their thoughts turn toward Bethlehem, the Christ child, and Christmas Day. My hope is that these chapters will also be beneficial to people seeking reading material to enhance their individual journeys toward Christmas.

Words of appreciation are in order to the members of my family—immediate and extended. These are the people who never allowed me to lose sight of the central truth of Christmas. My wife, Judy, and our two sons, John Paul and James, have been my best and most influential teachers on how to move from theology to festivity.

What follows is neither the first word nor the last word on Advent. It is only another word about the Word. The book is offered with the sincere hope that readers will be encouraged to prepare for a celebration of Christmas that is epitomized by welcoming Christ—the Savior who first arrived as a baby—into their lives.

—C. Welton Gaddy

INTRODUCTION

"Prepare the way of the Lord"
(Isa. 40:3; Luke 3:4)

*T*o observe Advent is to obey the Word of God that was shouted in the desert and recorded in the Bible, and how we do need Advent!

We have been keeping watch over our flocks and businesses and maintaining our routines by night and by day without any heavens-rending interruptions.

Heralds of good tidings of great joy have been as scarce in our land as reasons for rejoicing have been sparse in our hearts. Tears of loneliness and sadness have run unencumbered down our placid faces— faces devoid of those subtle lines caused by smiling or the deep, pleasant lines created by laughing. Demands and debts have far outnumbered gifts.

How we do need Advent!

So much time has passed since we last heard any angels singing. Night after night have come and gone without any stars shining above us, much less one bright luminary appearing to lead us.

Great is the distance that separates us from a happy pilgrimage to Bethlehem or to participation in any kind of festive journey of gladness.

We need Advent.

Now it comes—the season. Now He comes—the Person. Just when we may have thought God had forgotten us, if not forsaken us, we hear again that God remembers us and visits us.

Even as we may assume God is absent from us, we are made aware of God's presence with us. Heaven is near to earth. Eternity has broken into time.

Advent is here! Take a good look at it.

The Advent Situation

(The Human Context of God's Action)

Our first reaction to Advent may not be our best reaction. As we listen to the announcement of Christ's birth, ponder the meaning of God's inbreaking kingdom, and stare at outbursts of great joy, we may end up scratching our heads and mumbling to ourselves about our inability to put it all together. Advent comes to...

A Mixed-up World

We periodically experience moments of intense dedication, profound hopefulness, strong integrity, and heroic ethical behavior. But more pervasive, at times almost smothering, are instances of moral compromise, hopelessness, despair, and wrongdoing. During Advent our hearts are lifted by angelic voices singing of "peace on earth." Then on our hands are traces of the heavy black ink used to print newspaper headlines about an economy in trouble, a new outbreak of violence in the Middle East, and a dramatic increase in domestic crimes. Friends and family members have lost jobs. Crimes threaten our properties. That world seems terribly remote from the world which is envisioned in our hearts.

The birth of the Savior is thus welcomed with happiness. The coming of God's kingdom is viewed as a gift of great hope. Our spirits are buoyed by the promise of life everlasting. But children keep getting abused, friends keep dying, tragedies keep happening, and our questions about life become more and more difficult. Despair develops and deepens. Sooner or later we begin to feel like a juggler at the circus. We try to keep it all going at once—the despair and the hope, good news and bad news, lostness and salvation.

In a sanctuary, engrossed in worship, we know the future has dawned. The birth of Jesus marks the beginning of a new age. Paul's words express our thoughts, "Live like people who belong to the light. Have nothing to do with the,... things that belong to the darkness" (Eph. 5:8, 11, GNB). But the present is too much with us. We may not live in a home dedicated to worship. We spend the majority of our waking moments in an office or some other place of labor where some of our colleagues have forgotten all about

Christ and the better way to life He offers, where others have never even heard of such a thing, and where most people say, "just take care of business."

The poetry of Christmas is perfect for carols, nativity dramas, and children's programs. But it may seem out of place. We are more accustomed to prose than to poetry. Most of us are more familiar with the ticker tape from Wall Street that challenges us to decide on the best moment to buy or sell, not angels in the heavens that invite us to make resolutions about gifts. Peace is an ideal which must be set alongside the realities of competition and retaliation.

Our world is mixed up. However, it is the context within which Advent always arrives—the situation in which God acts. The joy of Advent is of sufficient substance to survive in a mixed-up world. Emil Brunner was gripped by that truth when he suggested that perhaps a storm lantern, not a candle, was the best symbol for Advent joy. Candles can be blown out too easily. The joy of Advent is strong.

Christ came once amid chaos and confusion, and He can do it again. Christ comes to our mixed-up world. He comes to us seeking a place in our lives. That is the truth of both Advent and Christmas. Advent, though, announces that truth recognizing full well the necessity of waiting. Another dimension of the Advent situation is . . .

A Waiting World

How often have we heard the words, "Hurry up and wait." We wait for birthdays, a driver's license, engagements, weddings, new jobs, children, promotions, opening curtains, and arriving airplanes. We wait for peace, hope, love, and salvation. To live is to wait. We seem to be forever looking forward. Ours is an Advent situation.

And how do we wait? Some people wait passively with their hands folded in silent prayer. They are waiting for a better moment. Meditation will have to do for now. Other folks wait with charts and crayons in hand—drawing lines, scheming schemes, and setting dates for the end of time (dates that Jesus refused to set).

We even see people waiting on television. Many people enjoy the annual fall television presentation of Charles Schultz's cartoon about Charlie Brown and the Great Pumpkin. Frankly, that program always makes me a little uneasy and stirs a bit of sadness within me. Charlie looks like a fool squatting in the pumpkin patch, crying out for the Great Pumpkin to come, and telling himself that if it doesn't happen this year it will happen next year. Charlie is waiting, but his waiting is futile, endless. The Great Pumpkin is not coming. Ever! Everybody seems to recognize that fact except the little, lovable, round-faced boy.

Charlie Brown's kind of waiting is not the kind of waiting nurtured by Advent. We are not destined to a life of crouching between church pews and silently watching for the appearance of the Savior each year only to project our unfulfilled hope into a distant future. Advent waiting is active, not passive; oriented to serving people rather than preoccupied with speculation. The season of Advent arrives with the assurance that the Christ who is coming has already come. We are not to *wait* for the future so much as to *emulate* the future. To wait in a manner appropriate to Advent involves working where people live in need and ministering among people who hurt. After all, if we are serious about seeing Jesus, we should remember that Jesus usually appears among those individuals who inhabit the cow stalls of society.

The human condition coincides with the Advent situation. We live in a mixed-up world marked by waiting that at times seems endless. Do not despair. Lift up your heart. This is the world in which God acts. This is the world to which Christ comes.

No sooner have we voiced our needs to God and repeated the ancient prayer, "Come Lord Jesus," than we discover that God has acted in history and is acting in our world. Jesus has come. And Jesus is coming. Such realizations put us in touch with . . .

The Advent Spirit

(The Human Response to God's Action)

In one word, the human response to the birth of the Savior is, "Hallelujah!" *Hallelujah* means "Praise God!" If a person struck by the indefinable grace of what God did in Bethlehem cannot say anything else, "Hallelujah!" is enough. Hallelujah is . . .

Introduction

A Means of Approach for Advent

Set logic aside. We do not have to figure out the truth of this season by way of reason. Every element of the message runs counter to our culture—God loves all people, even those who do not respond with love; in the nativity, all of eternity is reduced to a critical moment in history; the majestic, omnipotent God of creation appears in the form of a vulnerable, cooing baby; self-emptying compassion is directed toward self-protecting anger; exaltation takes place by means of humiliation; a royal kingdom is established by one who constantly ministers as a servant; God takes on the form of a man only to be killed by the people who are to be saved. We do not need to make human sense out of the incarnation. Simply falling to our knees and bowing before divine Wisdom is most fitting.

A person can spend the entire season of Advent pursuing answers to one profound question after another, but that is the wrong approach. Chances are that most of us would not even be asking the right questions anyway. Jesus Christ is far too great to be totally comprehended by our minds or wholly held in our hearts. Jesus makes most of our questions irrelevant as He instills within us a new kind of inquisitiveness. The best preparation for responding to Christ's birth is to set aside our questions and to practice saying, "Hallelujah." Even if at first it is only a whisper.

Preparation is needed. Preparation for Christmas is the purpose of the Advent season, although our preparation for a celebration of the Savior's birth will not cause Christ to appear. Jesus comes in His own way in God's own time. The appearance of Jesus is an act of sheer grace. Jesus comes when God is ready and offers Himself to us whether or not we are ready.

Hallelujah epitomizes the spirit of Advent and the nature of the most appropriate preparation for it. We are in a realm beyond mere reason. Rigid schedules do not count. God loves the world so much that He sent Jesus to Bethlehem. The One who showed up there shows up among us. Christ can be born in our lives. Heaven can touch our community. Eternity is poised on the edge of our society ready to penetrate our existence. What else other than to speak a hallelujah can be done as we prepare to celebrate the birth of the Savior? Besides, hallelujah is . . .

A Type of Commitment in Advent

Once people realize what God has done and is doing, what God has given and gives, whispered hallelujahs of preparation for Christ's birth are likely to become spoken declarations of reception—a reception of Christ. Adequate preparation for Christmas almost invariably leads to a joyous reception of the Savior. At that point, hallelujahs are unstoppable.

Look closely at the infancy narratives in the New Testament. Everybody who had anything to do with Jesus' birth eventually expressed unhindered praise. Zechariah, a stately old priest, skipped around singing like a feisty young minstrel. Mary was ecstatic as she lifted her voice in song. From the heavens, angels harmonized in a cosmic carol. Anna and Simeon, slowed by the wear of many years, saw the baby Jesus and began to praise God with an excitement usually found only among small children.

What else could be the proper response to purely selfless love? A hallelujah is hard to beat. The hallelujah which is whispered across our lips as we prepare for a celebration of the Christ event becomes a hallelujah in our hearts as we open our lives to receive the Christ child. God draws near to us in Christ. Hope can be reborn. Life can take on new meaning. What began as a whisper grows stronger. Surely God's commitment to us as revealed in the gift of Jesus will be greeted by our commitment to God as recognized in Christ.

One Sunday morning in Sighisoara, Romania, with my wife and a group of other people, I walked the cobblestones of that ancient walled city. At the end of the street which led from the center of town stood the wooden entrance to a long series of steps ascending the side of a huge hill. The steps were covered so they could be used in all kinds of weather. We had been told that an old church building stood atop this hill overlooking the city.

Nearly three weeks of constant meetings and travel in Eastern Europe had left me tired and homesick. I had no desire to climb 180 steps straight up the side of a mountain just to see another rough-hewed building, even though this one dated back to 1340. However, I started up the steps with the others. Near the top of the climb I heard a sound that seized the attention of my ears and stabbed at my soul. I could hear an organ—a mighty pipe organ—

filling the air with the melody of a magnificent hymn of praise. My pace increased.

I reached the end of the steps and climbed over some rocks to walk alongside the old church building. Just then the organ swelled, and I heard the most marvelous outburst imaginable of a congregational exclamation: "Hallelujah! Hallelujah!"

There in that strange land, a good bit tired, a little bit depressed, a whole lot disturbed, I heard a sound that set my heart to pounding and my soul to soaring. Hallelujah! Fatigue vanished. Excitement erupted. My spirit lightened. Hallelujah indeed.

My personal experience in Romania provides a crude analogy to our corporate involvement with Advent. Often we start this seasonal journey of preparation with fatigue, dread, and perhaps a small degree of cynicism. From almost anywhere we find ourselves, a climb is necessary to get to Christmas. If we stay with it, though, eventually we are surrounded by the glorious sounds that accompany Christ's nativity.

Like most analogies, this one breaks down. In Sighisoara, if I had not kept climbing the hill, I would have missed the hallelujahs. During Advent, though, before we reach the pinnacle of our trek up the mountain, we meet Christ coming down to meet and to greet us. Jesus comes down the "up" stairway. He comes to us. Heaven touches earth. We give ourselves to Him with a spoken hallelujah.

But that is not the end of anything. Rather, it is the beginning of everything. Hallelujah is...

A Pattern of Response to Advent

The whisper of preparation that eventually becomes a spoken declaration during Advent is destined to take the form of a sustained shout. The Advent Christ appears and all who see Him shout, "Hallelujah!"

Hallelujah is more than a commentary on this particular time of the year. It is a lifelong response to the incarnate God. What begins during Advent lasts forever. Emotions are set on edge with a sharpness that refuses to be dulled. Sensitivity is heightened to a degree that compassion recognizes and readily responds to almost imperceptible needs. Even the shyest of people can voice a hallelujah when they think of the birth of Jesus. Once a person has said it—really said, "Hallelujah!"—she cannot keep the word off her mind or in her mouth.

If an observance of Advent teaches us nothing else, it sets before us the truth that life is not a cut-and-dried affair. To catch the truth of Advent is to resolve to stay flexible—ready to do the unexpected, to travel an uncharted course—in order to be true to ourselves and faithful to God. Hallelujah is a life-style as well as a word. Hallelujah is a way of perpetually responding to the good news which occupies the heart of Advent—Jesus Christ is born.

People serious about observing Advent and moving on to Christmas must be willing to start a day's work and, if summoned, drop everything in order to go to some Bethlehem and worship at a manger. We cannot afford to delay the start of this journey until quitting time. The love that makes Advent possible elicits an immediate response. With a shout, "Hallelujah!," we sojourn to the site of the Savior's birth, whenever and to wherever He invites us.

Admittedly, to live like this is risky. A certain amount of vulnerability comes with being flexible and receptive, but with that vulnerability comes love, purpose, joy, meaning, and fulfillment. Each goes with the others.

No one learns the whole truth during Advent, although a fuller truth is not far behind. Christmas comes quickly, even if responding to Christ in joyful love gets us in trouble—and it can do that—even if it gets us nailed to some cross—and it can do that—we will be unable to refrain from declaring, "Hallelujah!"

God placed the words in the mind of John the Baptist. In good time this somewhat strange-looking prophet pushed them across his parched lips for those around him to hear. Finally the words formed a shout in the desert that caught the attention of everyone: "Prepare the way of the Lord" (Mark 1:2). Advent is our response to those God-breathed, John-screamed words.

How we do need Advent! We have waited for something positive to happen. Our souls have ached to hear good news. Now here it is. Advent has arrived. Incredibly good news is heralded to all people, and it helps us get everything in perspective. In our trek through history, we have stumbled upon a manger. Here we discover a baby crying, a father smiling, a mother laughing, and a strange assortment of onlookers rejoicing. Jesus Christ is born!

Excitement wells up within us until we feel like we will explode. Deep in our souls there is the rumble of a hallelujah that is rushing to become a shout. But suddenly we catch ourselves. We look over our shoulders to see if anyone is looking at us or listening to us. Questions trouble us, "Is this proper? Is this any way for a sophisticated believer to act? What will people think of us if we go around singing or saying, 'Hallelujah'? Even if it is Advent?"

We cannot deny the season or its earth-shaking message. The hallelujah is within us like lava spewing forth from the mouth of a volcano. Again we glance back over our shoulders. We shuffle our feet nervously. "What will people think?" We cannot shake our self-consciousness.

Maybe all we can do is whisper, "Hallelujah," ever so slightly so that no one else hears. That is all right. A quiet hallelujah is enough, a good way to begin the season of Advent. Stay with it, though. Do not lose sight of the season's major purpose and central truth. Before Advent is over, most likely, things will change. Standing before the newborn Savior we well may find ourselves able to shout, "Hallelujah!," without even looking over our shoulders or caring what others think. For the present, we best look realistically at where we are, confess our human condition, and focus our gaze on God's revelation. If we are ready to shout a response of commitment, fine. Let it go. Shout it out. But, if not, if a whispered hallelujah is all we can offer, that is all right, too.

What is most important is the fact that once again it is Advent! Christmas is not far behind. Thanks be to God. Hallelujah!

PART I

ADVENT AND CHRISTMAS:

Seasons of Worship

CHAPTER 1

A Personal
Pilgrimage

*C*hristmas Day is like no other day. It always has been the best day of the year for me. Every year, without exception, Christmas arrives too slowly, and it is over too quickly.

As for Advent, though, only in my adult years has this season had great meaning for me. Any meaning at all actually. During my growing-up years, I did not even know the term *Advent* much less understand the significance of the four-week period that it embraced.

My family had strong Christmas traditions. Approximately two weeks prior to Christmas Day, armed with a saw and an ax, we hiked into the woods to cut a Christmas tree. Each year the chosen tree was brought home, shaped up a bit, and nailed to two pieces of wood on which it would sit as long as it remained in the living room of our home. Decorations were added to the tree, usually on a Saturday. A few other Christmas decorations were retrieved from the attic, dusted off, and displayed throughout the house.

"Putting up the tree" signaled that it was time to buy presents. One evening of shopping with each parent was the general rule. Seldom did purchasing gifts require over two excursions into the local stores.

To begin these preparations sooner than two weeks before Christmas, three at the most, was unthinkable. A Christmas parade on Thanksgiving weekend was deemed inappropriate. Starting to decorate for Christmas early in December was considered "pushing it" or "overdoing it." Family members and their friends were often heard commenting, "People just keep starting on Christmas earlier and earlier each year. It is getting ridiculous. Christmas is losing its meaning."

Our church was on about the same schedule as our home when it came to getting ready for Christmas. An unspoken assumption was that to begin to talk about Christmas too early was to participate in commercialization and other abuses. Thus, in our congregation, Christmas carols, sermons, and lessons were limited to that same two-week period.

Worship services in our church were the same as they were every other week of the year. Only three items were noticeably different around Christmas. A large tree was decorated, lighted, and set in the front corner of the sanctuary (most people called this room "the auditorium"). Two or three pieces of special Christmas music were presented by the choir. (No *cantatas* or *oratorios*. Our folks smirked even at a mention of those words.) Finally, a children's pageant was put together in about a week and presented at the conclusion of a Sunday evening service or perhaps on the Wednesday evening immediately prior to Christmas Day.

Both in my church and my home, Christmas was recognized as a day of great spiritual significance. We complained about people who wrote "Xmas" rather than "Christmas." Excessive spending on gifts was discouraged so more money could be given to the church in support of foreign missions. From parents, Sunday School teachers, and pastors came impassioned pleas to remember that the meaning of this special season came from the birthday of Jesus.

When I finally discovered the meaning and value of Advent, I regretted that I had not known about Advent sooner. For me, this season met spiritual needs related to Christmas that previously had gone unmet and created a capacity for celebrating the Savior's birth that I had not experienced before. An observance of Advent can be a tremendous enhancement to a church's worship, to a Christian's spirituality, and to celebrations of Christmas in both individuals and churches.

The church family in which I grew up and among whom my faith was nurtured was set squarely within the Free Church tradition, with an emphasis on freedom. This congregation was fiercely independent, although it was a giving and cooperating member of the Southern Baptist Convention. The most radical antiliturgical elements of the Reformation lived on in this fellowship. However, the people did not want to be known as Protestants, only as Baptists.

In public worship, anything even remotely considered "high church" was unacceptable. Symbols were suspect. To speak of "Christian symbols" was to use terms that were considered antithetical. (Strange. The American flag, a civil symbol, was appreciated without question. Late in December, so was a Christmas tree—a symbol more secular than religious.) Ritualism and formalism were scorned.

From the indoctrination that occurred during my almost twenty years in that congregation came a worship-related suspicion that surfaced quickly when I was first asked to help another church observe Advent. Advent sounds "high church." Advent involves symbols. Advent is a part of the Christian year, a concept that hints at form if not ritual. My suspicion produced hesitation rather than cooperation, at least at first.

Is Advent valuable to Christian experience? Or should it be rejected outright? Does Advent contribute to the importance of Christmas or does it compromise that importance? Is there anything involved in Advent observances contradictory to the teachings of the Bible? Those were questions I had to answer.

Here is a brief summation of a portion of what I have discovered about Advent, Christmas, and the relationship between the two.

CHAPTER 2

The Background of Christmas and Advent

*C*an you imagine a year without Christmas? Of course not. But lots of them have occurred.

The birth of Jesus was not celebrated the year after He was born or even the year after His crucifixion-resurrection. In fact, for three hundred years after Jesus' ministry on earth, observances of the birth of the Savior were sporadic at best. Occasional celebrations were held on dates that varied from January to May.

History

Early Christians lived in a predominately pagan world. Pagan festival periods provided them with the best opportunities to conduct Christian celebrations, Christmas included. Often the themes, interests, and symbols of these nonreligious events were appropriated as means for expressing the nature and meaning of Jesus.

For example, non-Christians interested in the perpetual conflict between darkness and light were drawn to Jesus' identity as the "Light of the world" and the "Sun of righteousness."

Exactly when Christmas became an acceptable festival for most Christians cannot be determined with certainty. Evidence is that by A.D. 336 Christmas had been made a part of the Christian year, a twelve-month calendar of special days and emphases intended to take the church through the story of redemption.

Later, in A.D. 354, a bishop by the name of Liberius decreed that observances of Christmas Day should always take place on December 25. In the year A.D.

529, Emperor Justinian declared December 25 a civil holiday on which no work was to be done.

Celebrations of Christmas were held each year. However, the centrality of the Christ event was not always apparent. Enthusiasm and joy reigned, but neither was necessarily related to the coming of the Savior. Over the years, observances of Christmas became more and more chaotic. Finally, in the mid-seventeenth century, the Puritans officially banned celebrations of Christmas and declared Christmas Day a time for fasting.

Advent as a season of preparation for the celebration of Christmas had been started by Christians seeking to combat the pagan practices that were demeaning and destroying the religious significance of Christmas Day. Christian missionaries had been the first to set aside such a period. For many years, Christians had observed an extended period of preparation prior to the celebration of Christ's resurrection on Easter. Believing that annual celebrations of the birth of the Savior deserved no less attention and preparation, Christians started observing Advent. In the year A.D. 567, the Council of Tours established Advent as a season of fasting prior to Christmas Day.

Early observances of Advent varied in length. Some lasted three weeks and others involved as many as seven.

In A.D. 581 church officials set aside a forty-day period for Advent. Later, a decision was made to shorten the season. Advent begins on the Sunday closest to November 30 (known by many as Saint Andrew's Day) and includes no more than the four Sundays prior to Christmas Day.

Historians agree that Advent was the major factor in bringing about a recovery of Christmas as a primarily religious celebration. Amid the many powerful pressures to divert people's attention from the birth of Christ during the Christmas season, Advent observances can be of tremendous benefit.

People can be guided through the morass of secularization now surrounding Christmas and brought to focus on the advent of the incarnate God at a place called Bethlehem. The joy found beside the manger is unlike any emotion that is whipped up by storewide sales, television specials, holiday galas, or any other event.

Traditions

Christmas celebrations abound with traditions. Exchanging gifts, decorating evergreen trees, displaying colorful lights, burning candles, hanging greenery, sending cards, singing carols, and lighting a Yule log are now as much a part of our culture as of our Christian heritage. Several of these traditions have their source in ancient pagan festivals, but all were incorporated into Christian celebrations after Christian meanings had been assigned to them.

Christmas traditions vary from household to household. Those traditions may be secular or religious. Unfortunately, as in society at large, often an indiscriminate blending of Christian and cultural traditions takes place.

Churches, too, maintain traditions related to Christmas. Each congregation has its favored practices. In one church the decorations have to be the same every year. In another variety and change are prized. Public presentations of the New Testament's Christmas narratives by way of a "living Christmas tree" and a "live nativity scene" or a dramatic pageant presented for an entire community are increasingly popular. Almost every congregation sets aside time for at least one special musical presentation. Many congregations value a Christmas Eve worship service. Others gather for worship on Christmas Day (whether or not Christmas Day is a Sunday).

Advent traditions are neither as well-known nor as widely practiced as Christmas traditions, but they are no less valuable for people interested in maintaining the religious meaning of Christmas celebrations. Fortunately, most Advent traditions can be observed in either a church building or at home or in both.

Advent Wreath

Probably the most popular of all Advent traditions is the Advent wreath which originated in Germany or France. Numerous congregations and families have found an Advent wreath to be a superb aid to worship during the weeks prior to Christmas.

An Advent wreath is a circle of greenery usually containing four candles, one candle for each week of Advent. (Some wreaths contain enough candles to mark every day of the Advent season, but these are not common.) A wreath for the home is generally fifteen to twenty inches in diameter. Understandably, a wreath to be used in a worship center is made much larger for purposes of easy visibility.[1]

Three of the candles in the wreath are purple or royal blue (in a few instances red is used) and one candle is pink or rose. On the first Sunday of Advent one of the purple candles is lighted. The next Sunday, two candles are lighted. Three candles are lit on the third Sunday, and the pink candle is lighted on the fourth Sunday. On Sunday four of Advent all of the candles are aglow.

Many times a large white candle is set in the middle of the Advent wreath. This candle, known as "the Christ candle," is lighted on Christmas Day (or sometimes during a worship service on Christmas Eve).

The Advent wreath abounds with symbolism. Evergreens represent the gift of life and its accompanists the promise of growth and hope. The roundness of the greenery is intended to denote the never-ending nature of God's love. When three of the candles are royal blue in color, the regal nature of Christ is conveyed. If purple candles are used, the color commends repentance. The one pink or rose candle designates joy. (Among some people, the third Sunday of Advent is called Gaudete Sunday because the first word of the psalm for that day is the Latin *Gaudete* which means rejoice.) The whiteness of the Christ candle represents the purity of Jesus.

Perhaps the most potent symbol of the Advent wreath is one that takes shape over the entire four-week period. Light breaks slowly. Only one candle burns as Advent begins. The light intensifies as the season wears on. The brightening light is a herald of the coming Christ. On the Eve of Christmas, as every candle of the wreath is ablaze, people are ready to celebrate the birth of the One known as "The Light of the world."

When displayed in a worship center, an Advent wreath can enhance public worship. Each week during Advent, a part of the worship service is devoted to lighting the candle for that week. Members of the congregation participate. This particular moment in a service is a prime opportunity for teaching and learning Christmas-related truths. Generally, before a candle is lighted, an appropriate passage of Scripture is read. Often a prayer is offered. A carol can be sung by the congregation as the lighting takes place.

Variations within this tradition assign different names to the four candles included in the Advent wreath. A focus on some of these titles can be beneficial in worship. For example, the first candle is often called the Prophets' Candle. As this candle is lighted, comments are in order regarding the prophecies of the Old Testament, the pervasiveness of waiting among the people of God, and the manner in which the light of God comes into the world. Similarly, the second candle is named the Bethlehem Candle. While lighting it, the truth can be announced that the Christ who came to Bethlehem comes also into our world. The third candle, called the Shepherds' Candle, provokes thoughts of people who obeyed God's call, traveled to meet the Christ, believed in the Savior, and persisted in telling other people about Him. The lighting of the fourth candle, named the Angels' Candle, is a time for celebrating the love, radiance, and salvation apparent at Christmas.

My family has found meaning in and benefits from keeping an Advent wreath at home. The wreath is displayed in a prominent place. Traditionally, throughout Advent we light the appropriate candle prior to a Sunday meal. One member of the family reads a passage from the Bible. Another offers a prayer. Occasionally, we make an effort at singing a verse of a carol together, but we are much better at the reading, praying, and lighting than we are at singing. Christmas morning begins with the lighting of the Christ Candle.

Advent Calendar

Children especially may enjoy the tradition of an Advent calendar. Typically an Advent calendar consists of a piece of heavy paper covered by a colorful Christmas scene. Within that picture are squares representing every day of the Advent season. Each is covered by a flap that is not to be opened until that specific date arrives. Underneath each flap is the date of the day and often a verse of Scripture to be read or a suggestion for prayer.

Young children anticipate a new discovery on every day of Advent. As the dates on the calendar are uncovered one by one, everybody in the family marks their pilgrimage toward Christmas Day.

When our sons were younger, each morning of Advent in our

home began with a look at the Advent calendar. Before breakfast, the flap on the appropriate date was opened and the words behind it were read. Usually someone commented about the Scripture passage, prayer thought, or seasonal observation which was printed for that day. Also, invariably someone counted and announced the number of days remaining until Christmas Day. Not infrequently, at least one son would ask if we could look at some of the other dates on the calendar. Advent waiting is filled with discipline as well as joy.

Advent calendars can be made at home or bought commercially.[2] New editions are available every fall. However, some people, like those in our family, enjoy using the same calendar year after year.

Jesse Tree

Displaying a Jesse tree is a way of calling attention to the manner in which for years and years people waited for the Messiah in faith. The Jesse tree is a symbol of the chosen people of God looking forward to the birth of the Savior. This Advent tradition was inspired by the text of Isaiah 11:1.

A small evergreen can serve as a Jesse tree—either an entire tree or one branch of a tree—although live greenery is not required. A Jesse tree can be drawn on a heavy piece of paper or cut out of a sheet of cardboard.

In a sense, the Jesse tree is a family tree for Jesus. Jesse was the father of David, the great king who was such an integral part of the royal family into which Jesus was born. People who look at this seasonal symbol are reminded of the long period of preparation which preceded the Savior's birth and of the innumerable individuals who are a part of Jesus' family.

Decorations for a Jesse tree vary. Only four givens are involved. Whatever symbol is used for Jesse should be placed at the root of the tree. Symbols for David and Mary belong on the trunk of the tree. A symbol for Jesus should be placed at the top of the tree. A symbol may be no more than a piece of paper or some other type of decoration with "Jesse" or "Jesus" or another appropriate name written on it.

Family members can be creative as they construct decorations for the Jesse tree. Each piece added to the tree should call attention to some person or event crucial to the history of God's people prior to Jesus. Popular adornments for a Jesse tree are representations of the tablets of law, Noah's ark, Joseph's multicolored coat, and the harp of the psalmist.[3]

A Jesse tree helps us focus on the incredible diversity which characterized members of Jesus' family. God brought a perfect Savior out of a very imperfect lineage.

Chrismons

Chrismons are Christian symbols that are used to decorate a tree. The word *chrismon* is derived from the terms "Christmas monograms." In recent years, many congregations that place a Christmas tree in their worship centers have decorated this tree with chrismons rather than with more traditional ornaments that are devoid of any spiritual significance. A chrismon tree can be educational as well as beautiful. Every decoration brings to mind an important event from the life of Jesus, some image from His teaching, or a promise of the gospel.

Classes for making chrismons have become very popular in some churches. Interested persons meet together for several months studying the meaning of various Christian symbols and learning to construct replicas. Among the more popular chrismons are a manger, a shepherd's staff, the Greek letters alpha and omega, a star, a cross, a grain of wheat, a cluster of grapes, and a regal crown.

Often during Advent a church family gathers for a special service of public worship in which chrismons are placed on a tree. The scriptural background for each symbol is read. The meaning of each symbol is explained. A combination of music, spoken words, Bible readings, and the decoration of a tree forms a meaningful experience of preparation for Christmas.

In many churches Advent is a time in which financial gifts in support of foreign missions are encouraged. A missions emphasis can be integrated into a chrismon-related service very naturally. Many of the decorations have an implicit missionary meaning.

Hanging of the Green

When Christians first began to use greenery to decorate their houses and worship centers as a way of celebrating Christ's birth,

Christmas Eve was the appointed time for this activity. With the passing of the years, that changed. Today, many church families gather for a congregational experience of worship built around the hanging of greenery as a means of beginning the Advent season. Though not among the most historic Advent traditions, the hanging of the green is an act of significance in contemporary Advent observances. Often after a hanging of the green service, church members form small groups to decorate various areas of the church facilities. For example, a Sunday School class may have its own "hanging of the green" in the room in which it meets.

Worship centered around the hanging of greenery is an opportune moment for inviting individuals to commit themselves personally to a meaningful preparation for Christ's birth. A worship leader may say, "Let us ready our hearts as well as these rooms for a joyful acknowledgment of the Savior's birth and a personal acceptance of the Savior's presence."

Potential Benefits

Advent is filled with opportunities for spiritual growth, enrichment, and outreach. Each tradition of Advent is endowed with a potential for instruction and inspiration for the present as well as for important insights into the past. Small group gatherings, whether a Sunday School class meeting or an impromptu assembly, can study biblical texts for Advent, discuss personal problems presented by the season, and examine community needs that cry out for compassionate, redemptive action. Corporate worship during Advent embraces actions and truths that are media for Christian education, witness, and encouragement. An initial commitment to Christ and meaningful rededication to Christ are likely responses.

Consider a few of the potential benefits of an observance of Advent:

Biblical
God prepared the world and its people for the birth of Jesus. Hundreds of years were involved. Jesus came in the fullness of time. The Bible provides a record of that long-term preparation.

We, too, need preparation if we are to give ourselves to a proper celebration of the Christ event. Advent is the appointed time for making ready for a celebration of the incarnation. Through Bible study we can discover the ways in which people prepared for the appearance of the Messiah long ago.

Advent is a perfect time to reread, study, and reflect on Old Testament prophecies regarding the arrival of the Messiah. Ponder the settings of these texts, the nature of the hope that is evident in them, the substance of a faith that relentlessly reached forward, and the kind of activities that pleased the coming God.

The Old Testament texts of promise can be compared to the New Testament texts of fulfillment. In every instance, people's expectations of God's actions fell far short of the glory involved in what God actually did. All anticipation of the nature of the Messiah was inferior to the character of the Savior born in Bethlehem. Advent is a proper time for confessing that, in light of the truths of the Bible, we can never even come close to imagining the glory of God or predicting the nature of divine action.

From studying the Bible, we can learn how to wait expectantly, if not patiently. The Scriptures instill a confidence that in the fullness of time God will act redemptively. Within that confidence is the assurance that whatever God does will likely be beyond our wildest dreams and fondest hopes.

Doctrinal

"The word became flesh." "God was in Christ." The Divine became human. However the truth is stated, the incarnation is the central doctrine of the Christian faith. No one will ever comprehend it fully. Everyone should study it carefully. Advent is a season that abounds with insights into the nature of the God who becomes incarnate in this world.

During Advent, doctrine is taken out of the realms of the remote and the theoretical. Flesh, warm human flesh—not an idea or a conviction—was in the manger in Bethlehem. The baby Jesus who wiggled, whimpered, squirmed, and cried on that night of nights in the first century can be born in us and live where we live in this century. The incarnate God can show up anywhere at anytime. Whenever and wherever that is, there is the promise of redemption.

In relation to Jesus, all verb tenses deserve attention during Advent. "He is coming" is the cry with which the season begins. To take that statement seriously is to learn of the promise-making nature of God. God inspires the faith that God invites. Then, too, Advent underscores the announcement, "He has come." We know immediately that God is a promise keeper. As Paul the apostle pointed out, Jesus is the "Yes" to all of God's promises. With that realization comes hope. Finally, reverberating throughout Advent is the declaration, "He will come again." What has been will be. The One who came will come. Our waiting for the moment of Jesus' next coming is to be filled with the love revealed in Jesus' first coming.

People who engage the truths of Advent will know more than they have ever known before about God, themselves, this world, and the way in which Jesus relates each of these to the others. But it is not just a matter of intellectual insight. Faith is involved. And hope. And love. Observing Advent can result in a whole new way of life.

Evangelical

During Advent all of creation seems to focus on the Christ and to urge commitment to Him. Advent underscores the pivotal place of Jesus in human history. Time was split by the advent of God in Jesus Christ. All that matters most in life revolves around how a person relates to the Son of God.

People caught in the press and stress of the present moment suddenly realize, "We need a Savior."

What makes Advent and Christmas so special? Why do folk otherwise unaffected by anything make an effort to be kind, understanding, and compassionate during these days? How do you explain even hard-nosed competitors talking so much about peace at this time of the year? A partial, if not the whole, answer to those questions is the difference in life that is made when attention is devoted to Christ. What a powerful, persuasive, and evangelical insight.

Throughout December we hear comments like: "I wish the spirit of this season could last all year." "How nice it would be if people were so generous all time." The attitude behind those remarks indicates an opportunity to share the truth about Christ's power to affect a new creation.

To address the nature of Christ is to commend Him as the Savior. Consider, for example, a sampling of the titles that the Bible applies to Jesus: "Wonderful Counselor," "Mighty God," "Everlasting Father," "Prince of peace," "Light of the world," "Bread of life." Add to that list some of the various names by which Jesus is addressed in the music of this season: "King," "Lord," "King of kings," "Lord of lords." Little commentary is needed. The truth bears witness to itself. The appeal of Jesus is present in every announcement about Jesus.

Advent is about getting ready to celebrate a birth. Christmas is the celebration. But if the birth remains only an event in ancient history, the point of both is missed. The height of Advent preparation, like the epitome of a Christmas celebration, is allowing history to repeat itself—individuals allowing the Christ to be born in them.

Pastoral

Holidays are anything but fun times for many people.[4] In fact, holidays often drive some folks to anxiety, depression, panic, and despair. Advent and Christmas can do that, but it need not be that way. No seasons are more conducive to genuine pastoral care than these.

Images of Advent communicate an understanding of and identification with people in trouble—darkness, searching, waiting, longing. The message of Advent is that God is in these bad times as well as in good times. More specifically, God has the power to bring the best out of the worst.

Seeking hope, desiring joy, looking for good news, waiting for a breakthrough, and needing love are the stuff from which Advent is made. They also constitute the shared condition of a person lying in a hospital bed nervously waiting for the lab report on a biopsy, a young man crushed by betrayal and frantic because of a relationship that has ruptured, a single woman who for weeks has been unsuccessful in her search for employment, a couple whose oldest child has run away from home in a fit of anger, an older woman who has just returned from the funeral for her husband of forty years, and a college senior who has no idea of what to do about a career and fears even thinking about it.

Advent is for people on the verge of giving up. Its words of assurance about love, joy, hope, and peace have been born amid broken promises, tragedies, wars, and doubts. Neither Advent nor Christmas encourages a denial of reality and an escape into fantasy. Just the opposite really. Both seasons are sensitive to the harshness and hurts of life, but the message which they convey is that situations never become too bad for God to act in them and bring something good out of them. Isaiah stated the truth succinctly; "The people who walked in darkness have seen a great light" (9:2).

Advent messengers offer consolation and encouragement. "Don't give up." "God is still at work in this world." Retelling the story of the virgin birth is a means of communicating the truth that even a situation which appears totally hopeless can be the womb from which an unparalleled hope can be born.

One biographer of Dietrich Bonhoeffer describes the German Christian's winter in a Nazi prison camp. That year, the first morning of Advent followed a long night of bombing. However, as light broke, Bonhoeffer arose, prayed, and hung a wreath on his prison wall. Bonhoeffer knew the truth of the season—Christ comes to our kind of world; Jesus can be, and often is, born amid the bombed-out ruins of a city or a person's life.

Practical

Advent was begun to counteract the emphases and activities that accompanied the pagan festivals clustered around the Christian community's celebration of Christmas. Times, influences, and context have changed but not people's basic need for assistance in maintaining a proper focus on the meaning of the season. Advent can enable Christians to make their way through numerous distractions and arrive at Christmas Day ready to celebrate the Savior's birth and to demonstrate their life-long commitment to Him.

For many people December has become a dreaded sprint from one store to another by day and from one party to another by night. Gift-giving has been reduced to a chore. The festivities of the month drain energies and produce fatigue. "Just getting through Christmas" replaces celebrating Christmas as the primary objective of the weary.

Christians cannot afford to allow entrepreneurs, civic clubs, and partiers to set the agenda for these days. Christians have to be intentional and creative in their plans for the holidays. Advent is needed. Given present trends, Advent seems like a gift from God that can enable us to resist the forces which would erode the spiritual significance of the season, to preserve an emphasis on the centrality of Christ's birth, and to come to Christmas Day ready to worship Christ as well as to welcome Him to our world. Advent observances are important opportunities for people to catch their breaths, refocus their visions, and rearrange their priorities related to this season and to the One whose birth it celebrates.

Essential

Christmas Day is one of the two most important days of the year for people of faith. No other time provides more reasons for the meaningful worship of God.

Joy is the proper response to Christ's birth and every recollection of it, but not the kind of joy that shows up as a surprise, then subsides. The joy appropriate for Christmas Day is one that begins as a twinge of interest, develops into excitement, grows into a mature emotion, acknowledges the presence of problems, takes up permanent residence in a person's character, and persists amid great laughter and the flow of tears. Such joy is not automatic, a product guaranteed to arrive with the dawn of Christmas morning. This kind of joy develops only with time and patient waiting, the activity best learned during Advent.

What equals the incarnation of God in Christ? Nothing. Not anything! It is unthinkable, then, that members of the Christian community not devote themselves to the best possible preparation imaginable for Christmas in order to assure the most meaningful and joyful celebration of the Savior's birth.

CHAPTER 3

A Season of Worship

Worship is the proper work of Advent. God merits our adoration and praise. God welcomes our penitence and intercession. God invites our commitment and gifts. Always! But never more than during Advent. Our best response to the God who comes to us in Jesus is to present ourselves before Him and offer worship in Jesus' name. Our best preparation for the celebration of the Savior's birth is to persist in our adoration of the God who made the birth possible and sends the Christ into our lives.

Variety is important in the worship experiences that fill the season of Advent. Not all people have the same capacity for worship, just as not all people bring the same needs to worship. Some will want to join their voices in loud hallelujahs while others will prefer a quieter form of praise. A few individuals, plagued by pain and wearied by hurts, may want to avoid praise altogether. At the very moment one person is on the verge of shouting thanks for God's coming, another is struggling to keep from screaming aloud, "God, where are You? Why do You wait? Why don't You come into my world?" Some individuals will seek the music of one of the old master composers, feeling that only the classics can do justice to Christmas. Others will opt for more popular pieces of music, arguing that these better contemporize the birth. Advent has room for all.

Opportunities for meaningful worship during Advent include public services, family experiences, and private moments. All are important. No one of these is an adequate substitute for the others.

Public Worship

Few experiences of corporate worship are as powerful and influential as those that take place during the four weeks prior to Christmas. Bible readings are pertinent. Theology is practical. Good news abounds. The music is both intimate and majestic. Giving of ourselves to God seems to be the most natural act of which we are capable.

Pace, mood, and spirit are important in Advent worship. What happens with the Advent wreath points the way. All of the light is not there on the first day. Worship builds in intensity as the season progresses. Waiting is practiced as well as taught.

A temptation always exists to approach the first Sunday of Advent with tumultuous joy and bombastic praise. Finally, this wondrous season is here and Christmas is near. Great enthusiasm is understandable, but it is a mistake to give in to that temptation. Four weeks are ahead, then Christmas. A restraint of joy at the beginning will enhance the effusiveness of joy at the end.

Advent worship ought to reflect biblical history. Worshipers must not be allowed to take a shortcut to the manger, bypassing prophecies, hopes, and fears along the way. The movement of Advent is from pathos to promise to praise, from requests to remembrances to rejoicing. The season most fittingly begins with the haunting melody of "O Come, O Come Emmanuel" and concludes with "Joy to the World, the Lord Has Come!" Hurt embraces hope and moves to encounter salvation from the Savior, with a shout of "Hallelujah!"

Multiple media can be used to glorify God and to sustain the pilgrimage to Christmas by worshipers. Music is a natural. What can surpass the meaning and joy experienced through participation in a festival of carols? Sermons are important as well as appropriate, but there can be more.

Drama powerfully conveys the gospel narratives. Traditional Christmas pageants are still very much in order. The most meaningful are the most simple. Glitter, expensive costumes, elaborate sets, and other forms of polish seem as distracting from the story to be told as they do inappropriate to the kind of stable in which the story got started.

Dramatic monologues also speak to all worshipers, not just to children alone. For instance, on each of the four Sundays of Advent, a central character in the Christmas story, in period costume, could address the congregation. Worshipers could gain new insights into the struggles and the joys of people such as Mary and Joseph.

Many of the symbols of the season can be incorporated into congregational worship and can convey eternal truths. When a loved and respected elderly lady in a church, a woman who has endured more than her share of tragedy, stands before the Advent wreath and lights a candle of hope, only the most insensitive miss the message.

Storytelling is an integral component in journeys to Christmas. Among my fondest memories of Advent worship are those in which persons have shared their own stories as they relate to God's story. A woman spoke of her most cherished gift. A man talked about spending Christmas as a prisoner of war. A young child told of her favorite parts of the season. Nothing, though, surpasses a simple retelling of the story found in Luke 2. Often it is best told by a youngster filled with wonder, a child who is still discovering the story's glory.

Congregational involvement in worship is a must during Advent and Christmas. Worship is never a spectator activity, and at this time of the year every person's participation in worship is especially crucial. Members of the congregation benefit from unison readings of the biblical narratives. Everybody ought to be a part of relating the story of Christ at least once during the season. No one can celebrate Christ's birth for someone else.

Much of the music of these days is too soul-stirring to be assigned to a choir alone. Choir members can move away from their traditional position and stand throughout the congregation as everyone sings Handel's majestic "Hallelujah Chorus." To plumb the depths of Advent is to aspire to new heights and to desire to shout, "Hallelujah!"

When individuals of all ages are involved in leading public worship, everyone feels like a more active participant. A six-year-old girl offers the morning prayer welcoming Jesus to this world. A young woman soon to be a mother reads the words of Mary's song of joy and commitment. A teenage boy speaks a call to worship telling of his hopes for Christmas. For his going, a missionary reflects on the significance of Christ's coming.

Ministry is a form of worship not to be overlooked during Advent. Possibilities for service are almost endless. One act, though, can be of unrivaled significance.

Every community contains individuals who want to be involved in public worship but cannot because of age or illness. Members of a church do well to divide themselves into small groups, visit these individuals, and worship with them. Sitting in a sanctuary singing "Silent Night" can be a moving spiritual experience, but so can standing around a living room with ten or twelve children and adults, listening to a reading from the Bible, and joining voices in a somewhat off-key rendition of "Hark, the Herald Angels Sing," while gazing at an elderly person whose face begins to reflect the joy prompted by the infant Christ's arrival.

Advent is a time for focusing on Emmanuel—"God with us." Being with each other as the people of God is a natural response to a summons to Christmas.

Family Worship

Among Jewish people, Passover is the quintessential religious festival, and it is meant to take place in the home. A child asks why Passover evening is different from all other nights. An adult responds by relating the story of God's involvement in history. The model is of profound importance for Christians.

Within experiences of family worship during Advent, developments take place that would never occur in congregational worship. A child asks, "Why do we light candles before Christmas?" A teenager muses, "How do we know that Isaiah's prophecy has been fulfilled?" A young adult home from college wants to know the point of making such a big deal about this season. A young boy asks, "How does Jesus come to us?" Each question is an opportunity for religious education and spiritual growth as well as for enhanced worship, and a family member properly serves as a religious teacher, a spiritual leader, and an encourager of worship.

Family worship is possible regardless of the nature of a family's structure. A traditional nuclear family, a single parent family, a childless couple, an extended family that includes grandparents or an older aunt—all are appropriate fellowships within which to worship during Advent.

Family worship can be simple and brief—reading a passage of Scripture and offering a prayer. Or it can be longer and more involved—a fifteen-minute period that has been carefully planned. Each family has to find what is most meaningful for its members.

The Advent wreath is an excellent prompter in family worship.[5] Every member of the family can participate. One person can read a passage of Scripture. Another person can pray. Another can light the appropriate candle. Another can speak of the meaning of this particular source of light. Everyone can join in singing one verse of a carol.

Many years ago my wife formed, fired, trimmed, and painted by hand a collection of ceramic figures that make up a nativity scene. Each year that collection is prominently displayed in our home during Advent. However, the manger always remains empty until late on Christmas Eve or early on Christmas morning. Our family enjoys the tradition of one of us placing the figure of the baby Jesus in the manger as a signal of the end of Advent and the arrival of Christmas. This simple, practical act is in reality an act of celebration that takes on the nature of Christian worship.

Important also in my own family is a special period of shared worship on Christmas Eve. Usually, we invite two or three other families to join us for this experience. Everyone participates. Whether reading together the familiar narrative from Luke 2, sharing our prayer concerns, relating the Christmas events that stand out most in our minds, exploring the meaning of "Maranatha," or expressing our hopes for Christ's ministry among us, the words exchanged between us become the substance of a corporate act of worship offered to Almighty God.

If observances of Advent and other preparations for a Christian celebration of Christmas take place only in church buildings, a devastating assumption can develop. We may conclude that the spiritual meaning of this season belongs only to religious institutions. Every family and every member of every family needs to know that Jesus can be born in them in the place where they live.

Worship that is pleasing to God can occur in the familiar surroundings of a home as well as in a building constructed for worship.

The memories of Advent and Christmas that endure the longest are those formed within the context of the family. How good it is when worship is a vital part of what is recalled about family celebrations of the Savior's birth!

Private Worship

Before Isaiah preached to his peers about the coming of the Messiah, he encountered God while alone in the temple. In solitude, Zechariah heard a message from God that left him speechless. Mary received the astonishing news of God's favor for her with no one else around. Joseph, too, learned of God's will while alone.

Likewise, an observance of Advent is enriched by periods of private worship. The time and form for these occasions cannot be dictated. No person can tell another how best to worship God in private.

Some people prefer aids to worship. Private worship can be enhanced by reflecting on the meaning of various symbols such as the star, the manger, a shepherd's staff, or gifts. Daily readings from a book of meditations can give substance to an individual's quiet time before God. A hymnal is an excellent resource for private worship. Studying interpretations of the nativity by various artists can be inspirational. Parts 2 through 4 of this book embrace themes that can be studied by individuals during the four weeks prior to Christmas.

Honesty is an absolute necessity in private worship—especially in personal prayers. Subterfuge and pretense destroy the experience. For some individuals, times of private worship—with their invitation to honesty—are the most welcomed and cherished moments of the entire season. Everywhere else people go during Advent, they are expected to be happy and filled with good cheer. Alone before God, each person can state exactly what is felt and thought—happy or not.

Advent is a time for adoring God while waiting to celebrate the Savior's birth. In private worship an individual can speak of his love for God and the reasons for it. Voicing adoration to God will, no doubt, lead to expressing an invitation to God to join us in our lives, a perfect prelude to welcoming the Savior.

Another helpful exercise of worship is to compose a statement of greeting for the Christ child. How would you welcome Jesus to this world? What would you say to Him regarding His presence amid our lives? If you could take a place alongside the shepherds and bow before Jesus on Christmas morning, what would you say to Him? Answering these questions may take the entire season. Keeping a written record of your thoughts often proves to be beneficial.

While acknowledging God's gift-giving nature and preparing to receive the ultimate Gift, a person may wish to state before God the gifts she most desires. These usually consist of matters such as peace of mind, friendships, security, faith, love, and hope—items indicative of the reality of Christ's presence among us and within us.

Celebration

As a result of study, personal experience, and observations of the experiences of others, I am convinced of the tremendous value of observing Advent both in the church and in the home. My early suspicion of the season has given way to profound appreciation. I know firsthand the spiritual benefits of Advent by both congregations and individuals. I commend the observance of Advent without reservation.

For me, discovering Advent was like coming home. It still is. I look forward to Advent every year. I relish the odor of fresh-cut greenery and the scent of smoke rising from the candles of an Advent wreath. I exult in the tapestry of colors—red poinsettias, purple ribbons, crimson robes, white make-believe angels' wings. My spirit soars as a guitarist strums the chords of "O Come, O Come Emmanuel," a soprano hits the high notes of "O Holy Night," a harpsichordist accompanies a chorus singing "Go Tell It on the Mountain," a child hums the tune of "Away in a Manger," or an organist pulls out all stops and plays the conclusion to Handel's "Hallelujah Chorus." I am always excited about moving from darkness to light. I love all of that. But that is not the best part of Advent.

The pilgrimage is the prize. Every step of the spiritual journey to

Christmas is an opportunity for insight and growth. I discover that Mary, Joseph, John the Baptist, the shepherds, the innkeeper, and the travelers from the East are my spiritual brothers and sisters. They are also fellow pilgrims on this trek to Bethlehem. The nearer I get to Christmas Day, the faster my heart pounds and the greater my excitement grows. Preparation for celebration becomes a celebration in itself.

As Christmas Day dawns, joy explodes. Waiting ends. Receiving begins. Realization replaces anticipation. Hopes find fulfillment in flesh. Love is met. Faith is strengthened.

Do Advent observances take away from Christmas in any way? No, not by the farthest stretch of the imagination. Just the opposite. People who make their way through Advent in worship invariably experience Christmas Day with an intensity of celebration impossible apart from preparation, and the height of the celebration is a welcome. Jesus is greeted not only as the baby of Bethlehem and the Savior of the world but affirmed as the Lord of all life. "Mine included," each worshiper will likely be eager to add, "Jesus is the Savior and Lord of my life."

Hallelujah!

PART II

THE GOSPELS OF ADVENT

"Unto us...good news"

Matthew 1:18-25
Mark 1:14-28
Luke 2:1-7
John 1:1-14

Matthew

Matthew 1:18-25

The Conception and Birth of Jesus

*H*ow do you respond when someone says, "I told you so"? Or: "You should have known." "You were told." "They said it would be that way." Do you accept such statements graciously? If not, do these comments cause you to cringe inside and force you to exercise restraint lest you offer a retaliatory word or act?

Usually the context in which these statements are made affects the nature of their impact on us. Caught up in a situation fraught with great difficulties, an "I told you so" can be heard as a condescending preachment aimed at humiliating us while exalting the wisdom of the speaker. Conversely, in the midst of good experiences, an "I told you so" can be received as a supportive remark intended to encourage us by implying the speaker's confidence in us.

The gospel of Advent according to Matthew abounds with "I told you so" statements. The writer repeatedly declares, "All this took place to fulfil what the Lord had spoken by the prophet" (1:22), "For this is what the prophet wrote" (2:5, GNB), and "What the prophets had said came true" (v. 23, GNB). No negative motivation was involved. Matthew's intent was entirely positive. He wanted to express confidence in the message of the prophets and to encourage people to welcome the Messiah.

Matthew wrote primarily for Jewish readers. The New Testament book that bears Matthew's name is filled with citations of Old Testament prophecies and cherished hopes in Judaism. Having kept careful notes on how the ministry of Jesus corresponded to expectations from the past, Matthew was able to use concepts familiar to the Jews as a means of identifying (and commending) Jesus. In a sense, Matthew's entire message consisted of an "I told you so" from God. God had said a Messiah would come. God acted. The Messiah has arrived. Jesus is the One.

The good news Matthew announced to his peers is also for us. In almost every instance where Matthew describes Jesus as the fulfillment of an ancient Jewish hope, the fulfillment involves far more than was expected. God's actions went beyond people's fondest dreams.

The meaning of Advent in Matthew's Gospel is revealed in his identification of Jesus. Matthew's presentation of the incarnation is less dramatic than that of Luke or John. His words and images do not convey the stereotypical looks and sounds of Christmas like Luke's do, but the essence of Advent is here.

Details of Advent according to Matthew's Gospel are spelled out in the titles that Matthew assigns to Jesus. In every one, Matthew makes clear that long-term promises have been fulfilled in Jesus and that the nature of the fulfillment goes far beyond the greatest hopes inspired by the original promises. What tremendous news for Matthew's Jewish readers, and for us as well.

Two of the specific titles that Matthew applied to Jesus point to the general truth that stands at the heart of Matthew's writings.

Jesus Is the Son of David— but More than That, the Lord!

Throughout Israel the hope persisted that one day a new king from the lineage of David would be born. People longed for the appearance of a leader possessing the capabilities of their beloved former king. Jewish people were confident that one day another "David-type" ruler would ascend to the throne and elevate the status of their nation. However, as political situations worsened, that hope diminished. Fewer and fewer people believed any one man could establish international preeminence for the Jewish nation. Thus, Israel's hope turned to a focus on God's direct involvement in the people's plight.

Matthew begins his Gospel addressing that hope. His claim is staggering: Jesus is the fulfillment of Israel's hope for a king like David. To validate his assertion, Matthew does not point to a sky full of singing angels or a stable filled with lowing cattle and worshiping shepherds. Instead, Matthew announces the advent of Jesus by drawing a family tree. His statement is more matter-of-fact than dramatic, "The book of the genealogy of Jesus Christ, the son of David, the son of Abraham" (1:1).

A look at Matthew's work, a sketch of the family tree of Jesus, prompts mixed emotions. The promise of individual royalty is here, but so is the pervasiveness of human frailty. Matthew describes a heritage bountiful with both good and evil, an assembly of people in which the dishonored and the honored stand side by side. King David illustrates the point. David was an excellent national leader, but his personal life left a lot to be desired.

Study the family tree of Jesus. Matthew's description of the genealogy of Jesus contains the names of women. This is a major surprise. Few conscientious Jewish men, almost none actually, would dare include a woman's name in anyone's family lineage. Tracing the genealogy of Jesus, Matthew cites the names of four women. Each is controversial for reasons other than being a woman: the deceptive Tamar; Rahab, the noted prostitute of Jericho; Ruth, a representative of foreign blood; and Bathsheba, the unfaithful wife of Uriah and mistress and wife of David.

Jesus accepted the title Son of David. Prophecy was fulfilled. Ancient hopes could now be realized. But there was more. Not even the best of Israel's expectations envisioned all that happened when Jesus was born. Jesus is more than a distant offspring of the favored King David. Jesus is David's Lord. Jesus is more than a remote relative of royalty destined to exalt the nation of Israel. Jesus is God Incarnate, the means of salvation for all nations. Jesus Himself will be exalted.

More than the fulfillment of a hope, Jesus is the Creator of a new beginning for everybody. The Son of David is the Lord of lords. The kingdom introduced and inaugurated by Jesus will know no end. Hopes for a king were fulfilled by the birth of the Savior.

Jesus Is the Son of Man— but More than That, the Messiah, the Christ!

When speaking of Himself, Jesus frequently used a title that was intensely personal and immediately controversial. Matthew was mindful of it, and he used it often.

All well-versed Jews were familiar with prophecies about the advent of the Son of man. According to tradition, this figure was to be an individual representative of divine majesty. The Son of man was expected to be stern in judging evil persons and strongly supportive of God's faithful followers. No opposition would stand a chance of defeating him. Clearly the Son of man could not be a product of human planning. He must come from God, appearing as God's chosen one. The Son of man was to be the Messiah.

Jesus was the Son of man. Matthew was unequivocal in this assertion. More than once Jesus had used the title in a statement of self-identification.

Yet reactions to Jesus' acceptance of the Son of man title were mixed. The announcement fired hope in some people. Maybe the future was now. Among others, though, it sparked anger and charges of blasphemy. How could a carpenter from Nazareth claim to be God's chosen one! Besides, Jesus did not present the right image. He associated with sinners and remained aloof from members of the religious establishment. His words were inflammatory enough to incite a revolution. No one, literally no one, expected a Messiah like this.

Jesus *was* the Son of man. He was the fulfillment of a great hope, but He was more. One title could not define Him. During the same conversation in which Jesus described Himself as the Son of man, He spoke of the suffering and death that He would have to endure. *Impossible!* people thought. The Old Testament knew nothing of this kind of Messiah. Isaiah wrote of a Suffering Servant, and Daniel prophesied about the arrival of the Son of man. But no one dared imagine that those two would ever be found in the same person.

Jesus was more than anyone expected, and He gave more than had been promised. He was the Messiah, the long-awaited one. However, the reign of which He spoke knew no national boundaries. The kingdom that He announced had no temporal limitations.

An individual's political allegiance was not nearly so important to Jesus as were forgiveness for sins, the gift of hope, and a life of grace for all people. Jesus reordered popular priorities: life has meaning through service, losing one's life is the best way to find eternal life, and life's greatest victories come through what some people consider sound defeats.

Predictably, Jesus' words were challenged. His credibility was questioned. But His integrity was unmistakable, and Jesus' life confirmed His speech. Jesus was the Son of man as well as the Suffering Servant. Jesus was the Messiah, the Christ!

Other titles for Jesus also appear in Matthew. These two, though— Son of David and Son of man—were most pertinent to the mindset of the Jewish nation. Inherent in these identities for Jesus was good news for the Jewish people.

Of what significance is Matthew's Gospel today? We are familiar with the titles Son of David and Son of man, but neither seems very relevant to us, certainly not important. What is Matthew's continuing word of good news? What is the gospel of Advent in Matthew for contemporary readers?

It's there. Please do not miss it. From Matthew comes good news for us.

The Christ of Advent Unites Promise and Fulfillment

Past, present, and future intersect in the life of Jesus. Claims of God's mercy and might become present realities. The substance of a future-oriented hope is grasped by faith in the present.

The ministry of Jesus can be experienced now. His birth is a past event. What Jesus did in the first century, however, He is doing now: alleviating guilt, offering the gift of sight, nurturing wholeness in the face of fragmentation, providing comfort amid tragedy, initiating healing, making possible redemption. Such is the content of Jesus' present advent—an event from which all people can receive life.

Jesus brings into the present not only claims that had been relegated to the past but hopes that had been pushed into the future. The presence of Jesus is not a promise that we can appropriate only by hope. Jesus is here. Now! Redemption is available. Today! Eternal life is a quality of existence that can begin this moment. Life in Jesus Christ is a present opportunity. The Christ who came is here.

Look again. From Matthew comes more good news for us.

The Christ of Advent Demonstrates God's Abundant Grace

God is forever doing more than people predict or expect, giving more than people request or anticipate. Ancient promises would have been fulfilled had Christ come only to exalt the Jewish nation. But Christ came to elevate the worth of life for all people. Most folk would be pleased to know that the Messiah understands humanity, but Christ did more than understand. He understands us and offers salvation to us. How pleased most of us would be to know that Christ came to Bethlehem. However, Christ came and stayed—in a manger, in a carpenter's shop, in the temple, in the desert, in the Jordan, in the streets, in house parties, on a cross, and *outside* a tomb. Christ is among us.

God will not be, cannot be, limited by our expectations and predictions. Learn from what happened in the coming of Christ. In Christ, promises were fulfilled and more. Because of Christ, we live every day on the edge of surprise. Life abounds with God's grace.

Even that is not the last word, though. From Matthew comes still more good news.

The Christ of Advent Offers A Relevant Redemption

Matthew proclaims an incomprehensible paradox. Jesus is both human and divine. Matthew demonstrates that tracing the heritage of Jesus requires traveling a trail of sorrow as well as traversing a route of royalty. Jesus identifies with sinners and becomes involved in their lives even as He embodies the eternity of God.

Following Jesus does not take us out of the world but helps us find meaning amid our life in the world. To know Jesus, to relate to

Him redemptively, means to live with Jesus, in Jesus, for Jesus, and like Jesus right where life is at its toughest.

Jesus is with us amid our troubles to offer comfort. Jesus is with us in our struggles with doubt to offer faith. Jesus is with us under the threat of death to offer life.

Matthew is filled with good news for both Jews and Gentiles. Matthew's good news is addressed to his peers *and* to us.

Interestingly, Matthew ends his Gospel in much the same manner that he begins it. The message of Advent pervades the conclusion as well as the introduction of his written work. Matthew opens and concludes with an affirmation of Emmanuel—"God with us."

Promise has become fulfillment—"Jesus was born in Bethlehem of Judea in the days of Herod the king" (2:1). So there is another promise—"I will be with you always" (28:20, GNB). Jesus has come. Jesus comes again and again.

Advent according to Matthew is filled with "I told you so" statements of the arrival of Emmanuel—"God with us." For the Jews, it is extremely good news. And for us as well. From Matthew unto us comes good news.

Mark

Mark 1:14-28

Jesus Preaches in Galilee

Christmas was a very special time in the lives of the people who made up the open-country congregation which I served in southern Indiana. Every year Advent (although we did not use the term) included a program of children's music, a reenactment of the pilgrimage to Bethlehem by Mary and Joseph, and a staging of the nativity under a brilliantly shining star.

During my first season in that church, one of the good women in the congregation made several sets of angels' wings for the Christmas pageant. Though the wings were home-made, they really were something. Each was stark white and outlined in glistening silver tinsel. Just after they were made, everybody talked about the beauty of the angels' wings. The children wore them with great care. For eleven months out of each year, though, these objects of delight hung in the church attic. As you would expect, with the passing of time came the deterioration of the angels' wings. Amazingly, though, on the night of the nativity drama, with all of the lights out except for the one shining on the angels, those wings beamed with a breathtaking beauty.

Holy seasons and human traditions go hand in hand. Over the years, the meaning of an event which gives rise to a special time and the traditions which spring up in relation to that period become intertwined. Unfortunately traditions sometimes take on more importance than the meaning that the season was originally intended to preserve. Celebrations of an event take on more significance than the event itself. Often this happens with Christmas and the entire season of Advent.

Most people have Christmas traditions which they keep faithfully —sending greeting cards, wrapping packages in pretty paper, decorating trees, displaying candles and seasonal flowers, hosting parties, watching dramas, and singing carols. The stories about Jesus' birth are repeated frequently—whether the media are new or old, whether the poetic words of the *King James Version* or the more colloquial words of contemporary paraphrases. The Gospel of Luke gives us the familiar story.

Think of Christmas and certain images come to mind—a bearded man walking alongside a pregnant woman bumping along on a donkey, Bethlehem filled with disgruntled taxpayers, a crowded inn, singing angels, kneeling shepherds, and gift-bearing wise men. Concentrate on Christmas and familiar words spring into memory—"And it came to pass in those days, that there went out a decree from Caesar Augustus, that all the world should be taxed. . . . the days were accomplished that she should be delivered. . . . And there were in the same country shepherds abiding in the field. . . . Ye shall find the babe wrapped in swaddling clothes, lying in a manger" (Luke 2:1-12, KJV). We have heard the verses hundreds of times. Many people can recite the entire passage by memory.

Several years ago James Dittes, a creative thinker and talented writer, jarred my traditionalist thoughts about Christmas. Dittes pointed out an Advent account in the second Gospel of the New Testament, likely the first Gospel actually written.[6] I knew well Matthew's straightforward announcement of Christ's birth and affirmation that promise had become fulfillment. I also knew the philosophical-theological statement of Advent in John—"The Word became a human being and, full of grace and truth, lived among us" (John 1:14, GNB). But until I read Dittes' insightful work, I had never thought of Mark as the source of an Advent narrative. Now I am attracted most to Mark's message related to Advent.

In reality, the Christmas story in Mark's Gospel is so different from other biblical accounts of the nativity, so devoid of the traditional imagery, that some people say Mark's narrative is no Christmas story at all. Yet if Advent is about the appearance of the Son of God on this earth, about God's gift of the redemptive Christ to the world of sinful persons, then the good news of Advent is in Mark. The second Gospel can take its place alongside the other Gospels as a valuable source of information about what things were like when Jesus appeared. In fact, Advent according to Mark well may be an even more significant piece of good news for contemporary individuals than the Advent accounts of the other Gospels.

What Mark says about the appearance of Jesus does not include singing angels, kneeling shepherds, and gift-carrying visitors from the East. Instead of quiet pastoral scenes which conjure up images of tranquility, Mark confronts his readers with turmoil, a swirling social-political turbulence and a chaos in religious convictions which seem destined to construct a cross and nail somebody to it. One student of this Gospel observed that Mark's story begins with a wild man in the wilderness and ends with three terrified women running from a grave. Jesus first appears in this Gospel amid the turbulence of the wilderness, and His last words are a bone-chilling cry of despair from the cross, "My God, my God, why hast thou forsaken me?" (15:34).

What Mark communicates, in a way more poignant than that of the other Gospel writers, is that Christ comes to *our* kind of world. Many contemporary traditions related to Christmas almost relegate it to the periphery—a periphery which we enjoy looking at, talking about, and celebrating in some fashion, but once a year is enough because we must get back to "reality." As a matter of fact, an interested observer could be left wondering, "Can Christ appear apart from all of this? What if there is no hay, much less an absence of cattle, shepherds, and the like? Will Christ show up? Can Christ come into our kind of world?" Mark omits many of people's most favored Advent traditions in his strong assertion that Christ indeed can come into our kind of world.

What wonderful news! Jesus can come to *our* kind of world, and does. The Christ can be born in us—we who live where pastoral scenes have been replaced by asphalt-paved expressways, where shepherds have stepped aside to make room for men and women in business clothes carrying attaché cases rather than crooked staffs, where the quietness of most every night is interrupted not by musical angels but by blowing horns and screaming sirens. That is precisely the news proclaimed by Mark. Jesus can come also to us.

Many things have changed. The world no longer eagerly awaits a Messiah. In fact, most people are more eager to get rid of a savior than to accept one. Not many people today would drop everything on a split-second's notice and rush to the side of a feeding trough supposedly containing an infant king worthy of worship. Mark speaks to folks like that. Mark addresses the world which has changed, the world in which we live.

In Mark's account of Advent, Jesus appears not at the beginning of anything, as in Matthew and Luke, but smack in the middle of everything. No angels heralded the Savior's arrival. Jesus was first recognized publicly by a man whom everyone else considered deranged. The people who clustered around Jesus were mostly the sick, the poor, the abused, and the handicapped. Oh, there were a few frantic cynics who stalked His every step, disturbed by Jesus' ministry and resolved to bring it, and Him, to a quick conclusion. Rather than accolades of praise, Jesus received from His friends their studied judgments—"He is beside himself" (3:21). In Mark the Son of God receives no adoration, only the accusation that He is possessed by the prince of demons.

Reading Mark's account of Advent brings a deep sigh of relief. We may not like what we see, but we do know it well. That is the kind of world in which we live. There is a situation which we understand, a scene with which we can identify. Those realizations make Mark's proclamation powerful and profound. Not everything has to be in perfect order for Jesus to appear. Not everybody has to be genuinely receptive to Christ's truth for Him to show up in our midst. This is some of the best news which Christmas has to offer. Christ comes not just to Bethlehem but to my hometown and to yours. The advent of Jesus was not just an event of the first century. Jesus can be born in us today.

The Christ who without hesitation appears amid the chaotic conditions described by Mark is the Christ who can come to the world we know so well—to a world which almost daily gives birth to a new revolution, to a community deeply divided by prejudice, to a family fragmented by controversy and conflict. The Christ whom we meet in Mark's Gospel is not afraid to stand before an individual pulled in different directions by family and work obligations, doubts about career choices, frustrated that life has to be lived so much on the edge. Christ comes to our kind of world, to us.

Mark's message is certainly for me. My guess is that the same is true for you. We want to celebrate Christ's birth once more. But how are we to do it? How should we proceed? After all, not everyone stops to worship during this season. In December, life rushes on as usual, maybe even busier than in other months. Those of us who attend services of public worship during these days will have to fight the traffic caused by people going to shop. To maintain our priorities during Advent our schedules may have to fend off the demands of the very different agendas of our neighbors.

What is appropriate for Advent? How do we best observe this season? Singing carols and staging nativity scenes are fine. But that is not enough.

The most fitting way to celebrate Christ's birth is by welcoming Christ into our lives. Nothing has to be held back. We can open ourselves to Him completely. He will not be turned away by the pain, the conflict, the anxiety, the doubts, the frustrations, the disillusionment, and the guilt with which we live. Our problems do not precipitate any hesitation within God's compassion. Jesus will come readily into the lives of people just like us. That is what Mark says.

Yes, Jesus came to Bethlehem. However, the meaning of the advent of God could be missed completely if separated from the realization that Jesus comes also to us today. Jesus received gold, frankincense, and myrrh. Remember, though, Jesus gladly will accept whatever we have to give. Jesus came to a rather peaceful little village inhabited by people seemingly meek and mild in nature, but Jesus will not shrink back from the turbulence of today's communities filled with hard-hearted, strong-willed people constantly on the go.

Unless Christ is born within us, we have not experienced the Christmas event or celebrated the birth of the Christmas child. No number of pageants attended, carols sung, Scriptures read, or presents exchanged can make up for the lack of a personal reception of the Savior. And the news from Mark, the overwhelming truth from Mark, is that what is needed by us is offered to us by God. Christ can be born in us. In fact, that is the essence of Advent truth.

Jesus—the baby of Bethlehem—even now waits to be born in us. The Christmas event—the birth of the Redeemer—waits to happen in our hearts. So goes the gospel of Advent according to Mark. Unto us, good news!

Luke

Luke 2:1-7

Jesus' Birth in Bethlehem

On a cold February morning in 1809, two travelers met on one of the roads of Hardin County, Kentucky. The first spoken greeting between the two was a question, "Any news down t' the village, Ezry?"

Ezry replied, "Well, Squire McLean's gone to Washington t' see Madison swore in and ol' Spellman tells me this Bonaparte fella has captured most of Spain." Then came Ezry's question of greeting, "What's new out here, neighbor?"

The reply was, "Nuthin' a-tall, nuthin' a-tall, 'cept for a new baby down't Tom Lincoln's. Nuthin' ever happens out here."

Apocryphal or not, the old, often-repeated story underscores an incredibly important truth.

A testimony to the greatness of God is the divine ability to alter the course of history by the birth of a baby. Old Testament scholars have often pointed to the prominence of this truth in the Bible. The birth of a child marks the beginning of the patriarchal history (Gen. 12), the inception of the history of the nation (Ex. 1), and the beginning of the history of the kings (1 Sam. 1). When God works in history, not infrequently that work is associated with the birth of a child.

Projecting this biblical truth into the flow of human history, it has been declared, "When a wrong wants righting, a work wants doing, a truth wants preaching, a continent wants opening, a world wants a savior, God sends a baby into the world to do the work." A conclusion with ample justification is that as long as babies are being born, hope is alive.

The gospel of Advent according to Luke is built around the good news that a baby has been born, a baby named Jesus. Both miracle and commonality surround His birth. A mixture of the natural and the supernatural is present in the Bethlehem event. All of creation seems to rejoice over the miraculous birth of Jesus, though the whole thing took place in an ordinary stable. Onlookers spoke in whispers about kingship and a royal throne for the child while the baby wiggled and cried in an animal's feeding trough. Shepherds left their work and wise men traveled from the East to honor this infant, while a powerful king plotted to kill all the male babies in Bethlehem just to assure that the Christ child would never grow into manhood.

Revelation occurs when an event and the meaning of that event are united. The birth of Jesus is a divine disclosure. Words about this birth interpret the disclosure and fill it with meaning. Luke's message centers on an historical event and elaborates on its spiritual meaning. Luke reports on the birth of Jesus in Bethlehem. Then the writer explores the significance of that birth from the perspectives of Old Testament prophets, shepherds, angels, political leaders, and others.

Few people are unaware of the birth of Jesus as reported by Luke, but what about the meaning of the birth? How does the birth of Jesus differ from other births? Or does it? Ezry and his friend knew about the birth of Abraham Lincoln, but neither had any idea of the significance or meaning of that event. "Nuthin' ever happens out here." Is our situation similar to the one in Bethlehem? Is Christmas merely a fun time for recalling an event? Or are Advent and Christmas periods in which to celebrate a birth which is a medium of divine revelation?

Luke leads us to Christmas. He tells us about Christ's birth and contemplates that birth's meaning. Advent according to Luke is a narrative of good news.

Good News About the Particularity of God's Love

Perceptive men and women in the Old Testament often discovered that love is a dimension of God's sovereignty. Out of the pathos of his own life, Hosea provided a brilliant interpretation of divine compassion. Now Luke goes beyond all that has gone before. The Christ child is a specific example of God's love. What happened in Bethlehem is a tangible, irrefutable demonstration of divine compassion.

Luke's account of Jesus' birth and John's declarations of God's love are best read together—especially Luke 2:7 and John 3:16. "For God loved the world so much that ... [Mary] gave birth to her first son, wrapped him in cloths and laid him in a manger. ... This very day in David's town your Savior was born—Christ the Lord! ... so that everyone who believes in him may not die but have eternal life" (GNB).

God's love for the world is far more than an indefinable idea or a generalized affection. God's love has become specific. It is directed toward individuals. Stand before the manger, and you will discover that God's love is not just for the world as a mass but for every individual in the world. For me. For you.

The angel's announcement of Christ's birth provides a clue to the nature of God's love, not so much in what the heavenly beings said as to whom they said it. Shepherds were not favored people. Their work prevented them from washing often enough to meet the requirements of ritual purity. Yet the announcement of the ages, the good news of the birth of the Messiah, is delivered first to religiously impure keepers of sheep. What a sign of things to come. God's love embraces all people and each person. Not infrequently, God acts in such a way that religious outsiders see and understand divine love before religious insiders realize what is going on.

Jesus is God's ultimate Word about love. Truths implicit in the birth of Jesus become explicit as His ministry unfolds. God's love is for everyone. Literally, everyone. Jesus demonstrated God's love for the world, expressing God's love as readily to an adulteress, a leper, and a tax collector as to a rabbi, a priest, and a wealthy young man.

No one gets in trouble for expressing love for the world, for a city, or for a community. In fact, such a general love is considered admirable. The sentiment is noble. But controversy swirls when this love is brought to focus on specific individuals. Questions arise about the wisdom of associating with "those kinds of people." "You can love them if you want to, but you had better leave them alone."

Advent according to Luke is about a personal God not ever

leaving anybody alone, but loving everybody, all individuals (and all kinds of individuals) in an intimate manner. God's love made incarnate in Jesus is for sick persons and healthy persons, aggressive individuals and passive individuals, beautiful people and ugly people, the rich and the poor, white folks and black folks, yellow folks and tan folks, morally upright persons and unjust sinners, keepers of the status quo and iconoclastic revolutionaries, street people and homebound persons. Everybody! To stand before the manger and contemplate the birth of the Savior is to know that God loves the world, God loves all people, and God loves me.

Good News About the Nearness of God's Presence

In the person of Jesus, God comes near to us. How you say it matters little. The message of Advent is "God with us." All four Gospels declare this fundamental truth—each writer in his own unique manner. Perhaps Luke's pastoral, almost lyrical, presentation of the good news is best known—"to you is born this day in the city of David a Savior, who is Christ the Lord" (2:11).

The divine action at Bethlehem reverses the trend of traditional religions. Usually people search for God. The God who sends the Messiah makes that unnecessary. God takes the initiative. God reaches out to touch all people rather than remaining remote and waiting to be sought.

Strange things happened in response to the incarnation of love. Some of the people who had searched most diligently for God (or at least claimed to) did not want to find God or to be found by God when He was in their midst. Picking on the innkeeper in the infancy narratives is unfair. Virtually no one seemed to have had any room for Jesus. Not until Jesus arrived at Golgotha were people ready to let Him have all the space He wanted. Only on the cross was there plenty of room for Jesus.

The God who drew near to us in a manger in Bethlehem will never depart from us. That is a divine promise. We can count on it. God is present when two or three people get together in Jesus' name, when the bread and the cup are blessed and shared as Jesus instructed, and when truth is proclaimed. More than that, God is present when sin needs forgiveness, when anxieties produce a longing for assurance, when war causes a craving for peace, when death prompts a desire for comfort, when despair develops into a search for hope.

The God who comes to Bethlehem and takes up residence in a stable is not so preoccupied with the pomp and circumstance of the supernatural as to be unavailable in the natural. God—the God revealed in Jesus—lives where we live. God touches us where we hurt the most and joins us in rejoicing. The manger is only one place where a person can meet God. Look around. God is with us now, wherever we may be.

Good News About the Comprehensiveness of God's Redemption

In Jesus, the holy God of creation confronts us in the common garb of human flesh. Try to grasp the awe-inspiring implications of this truth.

No area of life is outside the scope of God's redemption. Salvation is available for everybody—not just for the pious who have tried to earn it but also for people who can do no more than gratefully receive it as an undeserved gift. Salvation brings strength to people in all situations—not just in high moments of corporate worship but also in low moments of vocational crisis, economic need, or personal tragedy. The relevance of salvation reaches far beyond the concerns of religion. God's redemption is for the entirety of life.

God's redemption affects my total being, and yours. God is not after our souls alone. God has acted to redeem our talents, conversations, economics, intellects, interests, politics—indeed, our lives. The results of this all-embracing, life-changing redemption are spelled out best by the apostle Paul: love, joy, peace, patience, kindness, goodness, faithfulness, humility, and self-control (Gal. 5:22-23).

God's redemption affects my relationship to other beings. And yours. God's redemption is personal but not private. The nativity of Jesus creates the possibility of goodwill and peace in society. In God's act of redemption there is a power mighty enough to tear down walls of separation, wipe out structures of prejudice, and build avenues for communication and understanding. As God redeems individuals, God creates the possibility of a redeemed community.

Privilege is accompanied by responsibility. Redemption is no exception. To receive God's gift of redemption is to accept a responsible role in the ongoing ministry of redemption. Even here there is good news. The nature of God's redemption is such that we are enabled to do what we are expected to do—God helps us to become the persons God wants us to be. We do not have to carry the backbreaking burden of attempting to be good enough to please God. God works within us.

The gospel of Advent according to Luke instructs and inspires us. Christ's birth is to be celebrated, but that is not all. The meaning of that birth is also to be contemplated. Neither is a task devoid of pleasure. Recalling the birth of Jesus and meditating on the meaning of that event provoke joy.

The news from Luke is good. "This very day in David's town your savior was born—Christ the Lord!" (Luke 2:11, GNB). God loves the world. God loves us—each of us, all of us. God loves me. God has come to be with us—each of us, all of us. God comes to be with me. God acts to redeem us—each of us, all of us. God acts to redeem me. This is the message of Luke. Advent according to Luke is unto us good news!

John

John 1:1-14

The Deity of Jesus Christ

*H*ere we go again! That is the sense of John's opening statement in his version of the gospel of Advent. Literally, John wrote, "In the beginning..." (1:1). Immediately, the words send the minds of all who read them scurrying back to the creation account. Note the accompanying emotion. John's terms convey joy, not despair. John sees the birth of Jesus as a new beginning, analogous to the first. The Christ of Christmas is the embodiment of newness and the promise of new beginnings. This biblical-historical-theological truth has an intimate personal application. Life can begin again. Because of what God did in Bethlehem, all people are given the opportunity for a fresh start.

In order to explore its meaning, John sets the Christ event in a larger context than do the other Gospel writers. He also used different terminology to describe it. John's Gospel is about God's coming to earth in Christ. An Advent narrative is unmistakable, but John's gospel of Advent relates the birth of Jesus to all people, not to one group alone.

For John, the advent of Jesus is no seasonal happening, no narrowly religious event, no closed-cultural experience. Rather, it is a cosmic event of redemption. In the same way that the dawn of creation was for the entire word, the birth of Jesus is for the entire world.

The sweep of John's Gospel may leave us wide-eyed and breathless. Its scope is so large and its promises so wonderful. John provides important insights into the meaning of Christ's birth. But more, he sets before us the essence of

Christian truth and instructs us on how this is to be shared with others.

The Explicit Truth:
God Can Become a Human Being and Still Be God

The most staggering statement in the Bible is John's declaration "the Word became flesh and dwelt among us" (1:14). John intended that no doubt exist—God took on human form in Jesus. The God of creation is the God of redemption. For God, greatness and humility are not mutually exclusive traits. No eternal stand off exists between the divine and the human. John's God, the God we worship, is no sky god who peers at the world from the security of a distant vantage point. The God we see revealed in Jesus is no uninvolved, unreachable, out-of-touch deity. God is among us. God has become incarnate in Jesus Christ.

John's message is troublesome for some people. To speak of God in human form, the divine Being in flesh and blood, is to talk of concepts that are difficult to comprehend, much less believe. However, John's words about God were probably even more difficult, scandalous actually, for those who read them first. Holiness had been equated with distance. Flesh and fleshly concerns were synonyms for evil. Only the spiritual aspects of life were considered good. John's announcement that God had become flesh incited rage among many folks who considered such talk sacrilegious and heretical.

John's word pictures are vivid. He uses terms that were associated with the Old Testament writers' concept of the shekinah glory of God—the image is that of God pitching a tent among us. God has tabernacled among people as human flesh. The incarnation is not a *symbol* of anything. The incarnation is a *real* event—an historical event, a personal event.

Throughout the fourth Gospel, John describes in detail the full humanity of Jesus. He presents Jesus as a man who becomes angry, grows tired, feels hungry, identifies with people who are afraid, needs water, and weeps. It's a paradox. The Gospel that places the greatest emphasis on the divinity of Jesus is the same Gospel that stresses most the humanity of Jesus.

Note, however, that God is not compromised by becoming human. Rather, God is realized in human form. The greatness of God is enhanced, not diminished, by human understanding. God is a personal, compassionate Deity—not merely a noble idea, an amiable goal, or a lofty concept. God can be known in the person of Jesus. God can be loved more dearly than any family member or friend. Never was the majesty of God more evident than when viewed in the humility and humanity of Jesus.

From the time of creation, God has let the divine nature be known by people. Revelation occurred again and again. Jesus, though, is the epitome of revelation. After Bethlehem, no one was left wondering what God is like. God is like Jesus because Jesus *is* God. Jesus showed us how God would live on earth, and how God wants everyone to live.

The gospel of Advent according to John provides insights into the incarnation that are of profound importance, and not just theologically. John helps us better to understand the nature of Jesus, but he also engages us with truths about the nature of our lives when we are in a loving, redemptive, obedient relationship with Christ. For example, consider:

The significance of flesh. God's incarnation in Christ administers a death blow to any philosophy that separates material matters and spiritual matters, making the former evil and the latter good. God looked at creation—the world, material objects, flesh and blood human beings—and God said, "Good." Jesus echoes that affirmation. In the manger at Bethlehem, the material and spiritual come together. "The Word became flesh."

Flesh is not eternal, but it is to be taken seriously. Our bodies have value as do our spirits. The human body is to be cared for and treated with respect. Sex is no filthy invention of the devil devised to cause the downfall of humanity. Sex is a good gift from God intended for enjoyment and procreation within the permanent human relationship of marriage between a man and a woman. Material items are not to be cursed as distractions from what is good but blessed as instruments to be used in doing good. "The Word became flesh."

The glory of humanity. Jesus is the supreme example of a human being. To follow Jesus does not require forfeiting humanity. In reality, following Jesus results in humanity being nurtured toward its divinely defined goal. To be like Jesus is to be fully human. God's desire is for people to become more human, not less. Humanity is not a flaw for which people must apologize. God chose to be human. Humanity is the medium through which we best serve God. That which fosters a true humanity is to be affirmed. All that degrades or destroys human worth is to be rejected. A right relationship with God involves a resolve to be all that God intended us to be as human beings.

The worldliness of salvation. God chose the world as the realm in which to work out our salvation. God did not stand outside the world and summon people to a meeting. God came into this world to mix and mingle with all people. And, according to divine directions, our service to God is to occur squarely within the world. Jesus sets the example. God provides the strength necessary for us to follow the example Jesus set. By means of the life of Christ, we are enabled to bear anything this world has to offer as well as to enjoy all that heaven has to offer.

John's words about Jesus' ministry describe a salvation meant for those seeking to live in the world rather than for those anxiously searching for a route of retreat. Christian redemption is a reality of life, not an abstract idea. The salvation effected by Jesus does not take people away from temptations, crises, and hardships. Instead, it empowers them to live through all of these. Life with God holds promise for the future, but never at the expense of ignoring the present. Eternal life as made possible by Jesus begins now and finds expression amid the mundane moments of this world.

The Implicit Truth:
The Gospel Can Become Understandable and
Still Be Gospel

From the birth of Jesus comes not only the message of redemption but a model for sharing that message. God comes to us in human form, yet remains God. Mystery becomes understandable, yet remains mystery.

The gospel is not made more sacred by making it difficult to understand. Interestingly, John's writing has been labeled as both the simplest and the most complex of the four Gospels. What a compliment! Legitimately, the two can and should stand side by side. Among all who share it, the gospel can retain its mystery without being made mysterious. In order for the gospel to do its redemptive work, it must be understood. Messengers of the gospel are most faithful to its nature (and to the nature of God's whole ministry of redemption) when they share the good news in a penetrating and understandable way.

John was captivated by the good news of the Christ event and wanted to share it, but a major problem stood in his way. The traditional religious categories of Judaism were inadequate for conveying the meaning of Jesus to John's specific audience. More Greeks than Jews would read his words. (Some estimates are that by the time John wrote his Gospel there were one hundred thousand Greeks for every one Jew in the church.) Many of these people were totally unfamiliar even with the hope for a Messiah.

John solved his problem by doing with the gospel what God had done with Christ. The incarnation is God's means of speaking the language of people. The whole point of revelation is understanding. John could do no less. So John's account of the advent of Jesus does not contain familiar Jewish titles for Jesus (such as those found in Matthew's Gospel). John calls Jesus "the Word." Greeks immediately understood because the idea of *logos* (the word) as a basic element of the cosmos had been part of their philosophy for hundreds of years. John took a concept familiar to his readers and filled it with Christian meaning. That is how he shared the gospel.

What John saw and did, we must see and do. The truth about Christ is larger than any language employed to share it. Gospel proclamation may employ a vocabulary that is Greek or Jewish, philosophical or colloquial, sophisticated or simple. The truth is the same. This insight is crucial to evangelistic and missionary efforts. The gospel must be shared in an understandable manner. Think what this means.

The gospel is not limited to a specific set of words. The gospel cannot be reduced to one phrase or one group of phrases, to one word or one group of words.

Some people seem to have the impression that sharing the gospel consists of repeating certain words. If those words are not present, the gospel is not proclaimed. However, that is by no means correct.

Well-known words like *saved* and *lost* may not speak to some people. Vocabularies differ among people. Terminology changes from generation to generation. If we speak only inhouse Christian jargon, how will the outside world understand the good news?

Gospel *truth* is greater than any one word or combination of words. Thus, in John's account of Advent, readers do not encounter Jesus as the Son of David and Emmanuel. John writes of "the Word" which becomes flesh. He means Jesus. Gospel proclamation takes place in many different forms. In the New Testament, the gospel is shared by means of preaching, singing, baptism, and the Lord's Supper. Today the gospel can also be communicated through the spoken word, drama, music, art, literature, and film (to name only a few media). The ministry of an evangelist for Christ may originate behind a pulpit, in a choir loft, at work, with a neighbor, in a broadcast studio, or in the makeshift office of a social service agency. John points the way.

The gospel is not bound to a specific culture. The gospel of Advent in John is couched in the language of Greek philosophers so as to appeal to a Greek mindset. However, it is a message for the whole world. God comes to scholars as well as shepherds, to philosophers as well as the illiterate, to traders in the marketplace as well as to worshipers in the temple. The advent of God was, and is, for everybody—all people.

The universal nature of the gospel became a point of contention in the early church. Jewish Christians wanted believers to become Jews before they became Christians. It was not to be.

The advent of God in Christ creates the possibility for all kinds of people to become Christians and to live as Christians within their own societies and cultures. Meeting Christ does not necessitate speaking a certain language or dressing a certain way any more than it requires being born as a member of a specific race. God came near to all people in Christ. All people can come to God through Christ.

Advent according to John is a message of good news. God's incarnation at Bethlehem embraces the day of creation, Christmas Day, yesterday, today, and tomorrow. God's presence in the world cannot be limited to a single season of the year. God's involvement with humanity reaches beyond the boundaries of any one community. Jesus is for everybody everywhere. God has come. God comes. God is with us.

John reminds us that the advent of God in Christ makes all of life significant. Christ can be known in the realm of the flesh as well as the spirit. The salvation made possible by Jesus does not exclude any dimension of our existence. Advent according to John is good news for everybody, for all people in all kinds of situations. Advent according to John is unto us good news!

PART III

THE LIGHTS OF ADVENT

"Christlight"

The Dilemma of Darkness

Isaiah 60:1-3, 19-22; John 8:12; Revelation 21:1-3, 22-24

Waiting for the Light

*D*arkness! The kind James Weldon Johnson described: "Blacker than a hundred midnights/Down in a cypress swamp."[7] Darkness is everywhere. In the words of the writer in Genesis, "Darkness was upon the face of the deep" (1:2). Primordial darkness.

Light! The kind God brought into being in the first act of creation. Brilliant, blinding, beautiful light. Light brighter than sunshine at high noon on a cloudless day.

Philosophers continue to study the struggle between light and darkness. Their speculations are as old as the most primitive, superstitious nature worshiper. Ancient religionists equated darkness with immorality; light with righteousness. Residents of the Qumran community made famous by the Dead Sea Scrolls wrote of the perpetual war between children of light and children of darkness. Rituals involving light were developed to warn of the perils of darkness and to attract persons to the illumination found in the commandments of God.

Christianity is uniquely concerned with light. Theoretical thoughts and ritual acts are not the substance of this concern, though. For Christians, *the* light is a person. Darkness is dispelled by a birth. Christians concentrate on the Light of the World sent from God to eradicate all darkness.

Advent is about the arrival of this light—Christlight. Journeying to Christmas involves adjusting our vision to the inbreaking light. But the pilgrimage begins, as does the gospel of Christ, against the backdrop of darkness.

Darkness Is the Human Dilemma

As a young boy Samuel stumbles around in the darkened temple, when "the word of the Lord was rare" (1 Sam. 3:1). Look at Job—his pitiable figure perched atop an ash heap profiled against a setting sun, sitting amid dying light. Hear the prophet Isaiah crying, "Comfort, comfort" (40:1) over the grumblings of people engulfed by the all-encompassing darkness of exile. Watch Judas get up from the table where he shared his last meal with Jesus and rush away to set in motion the arrest of Jesus. John wrote of that moment, "It was night" (13:30). Take note that, according to the Gospel writers, as Jesus screamed from the cross, "My God, my God, why have you forsaken me?" (Matt. 27:46), "the sun's light failed" and "there was darkness over the whole land" (Luke 23:44-45).

Biblically, darkness characterizes life without God. It is a precreation condition—"Darkness was upon the face of the deep" (Gen. 1:2). It is a preredemption situation—"men loved darkness rather than light" (John 3:19). It is judgment—"And cast him [the worthless servant] into the outer darkness" (Matt. 22:13).

Darkness is no stranger to us. Why does God seem not to answer my prayers? Why do innocent people suffer? What sense can be made of an incurable disease? Is there no end to violence between individuals and wars between nations? Why doesn't God do something about the mess in which we live? We know darkness all too well.

Some folks try to adjust to darkness. They accept a lack of light and resolve to live like bats. Often such people do not even look for illumination and guidance. Other people, though, know what eventually most people come to know. An individual cannot live in darkness and experience joy. Darkness destroys personhood one way or another.

Attempting to live in darkness is like trying to walk through a blackened cave. Each tentative step is accompanied by dreadful caution and a terrible strain born of the fear of plummeting into a bottomless chasm. Living in darkness is like walking through a room in the middle of the night and striking your shins on the side of a chair. Trying to function in darkness is like groping for a ringing telephone when you are unable to see what you hear.

Seeking to settle into darkness is like wanting to get away but fearing to run in the blackness of night. We want light. We need light. Desperately!

So we wait. We wait for answers to our questions. We wait for assurances to resolve our doubts. We wait for security to calm our fears. We wait for some sort of helpful intervention in our lives. We wait for a presence. We wait for light.

Waiting Is the Context of Our Hoping

Life is filled with waiting. A child waits until he is old enough to enroll in school. A teenager waits for that birthday that qualifies her for a driver's license. A high school senior waits with excitement for going off to college. A graduate student waits for a verdict about his dissertation. A young woman waits for just the right job offer. A man in his early twenties waits to get married. A middle-aged professional waits for a promotion. A weary worker waits for a vacation. An older man waits for grandchildren. A couple waits for retirement. A wise student of the meaning of life once suggested that when waiting ends, life ends. It does seem that way.

Generally, people caught up in waiting share a common assumption—the next stage of life will be better than the present. Then I will have answers. Then I will understand. Then I will know how to act. Then I will find fulfillment. Then I will be free. Then I will have more time. Then I can live out my faith more consistently. Then I will make a commitment. Then! Always then. We live waiting—endlessly waiting—always more on the verge of something than in the midst of anything.

Waiting is as difficult as it is common. Waiting wears on a person, wears out a person—sitting by a telephone waiting for it to ring so you can begin a conversation that may change everything; pacing up and down the hall of a hospital waiting for a physician to tell you the surgery has been completed; waiting for a client to respond to your last offer; forcing yourself to wait for your children to discover for themselves the value of honesty.

Waiting is worsened by darkness—physical, mental, or spiritual darkness. A parent acknowledges that she could wait for the return of a child if she just knew the child would return unharmed. A job applicant knows that waiting for employment would be easier if there were any assurance that a positive answer would ever be received. A hurting husband trying to wait out a storm in his family knows that his patience could be strengthened if he knew turbulence would end.

However, hope is born in waiting. Hope! Hope is born in waiting even if the waiting is in darkness. An exiled captive writes, "Yea, we wept when we remembered Zion. We hanged our harps up on the willows," (Ps. 137:1-2, KJV). "For behold, darkness shall cover the earth, and thick darkness the peoples" (Isa. 60:2). The picture is one of pathos. Waiting seemed interminable for enslaved people confined to a foreign land. Yet waiting in misery was the context in which the prophet Isaiah declared, "Arise, shine, for your light has come" (v. 1). Amid darkness, with eyes of hope, Isaiah saw more than a glimmer of light.

Centuries later John had a similar experience. Imprisoned on the island of Patmos, John was waiting for deliverance. However, in the midst of his waiting, John found hope. Confronted by a wall of darkness, the visionary wrote, "I saw a new heaven and a new earth" (Rev. 21:1) and "the city has no need of sun or moon to shine upon it, for the glory of the Lord is its light" (v. 23). John's waiting was filled with hoping.

This truth about waiting and hope, hope amid waiting, belongs to the present as well as to the past. Often hope is born at the moment darkness seems densest—when unanswered questions are no longer tolerable, when challenges appear insurmountable, when trouble becomes unbearable.

A mother found her young daughter drawing a picture. The small child explained that it was a picture of God.

"But no one knows what God looks like," the mother wisely counseled.

Undeterred, the little girl confidently responded, "They will when I get through."

Hear, hear! Shrouded in darkness, we may not know the precise shape of the fulfillment of the promise to which we cling, we may not have any idea of what God's presence will look like amid our difficulties, and we may be completely devoid of thoughts regarding the form of our deliverance, but we can hope. We do hope.

By means of faith, we can wring from the most threatening darkness a vision of light, and from that vision hope can be born. Handel, the great composer, incorporated this truth into his monumental work, *Messiah*: "For, behold, the darkness shall cover the earth, and gross darkness the people: but the Lord shall arise upon thee, and his glory shall be seen upon thee. And the Gentiles shall come to thy light, and kings to the brightness of thy rising."[8]

Deliverance Is by Means of Light

Official reports indicate that in England during World War II, more lives were lost because of the blackouts to prevent air raids than because of the raids themselves. Darkness was destructive. Darkness *is* destructive.

Everybody needs light. We seek light for our questions as well as for our paths. We long for lights at the end of all our tunnels.

In a way, Samuel Beckett's play *Waiting for Godot* is a parable. The fictional characters Vladimir and Estragon discover that their words to each other do not make sense and conclude that they never will make sense until Godot arrives. We understand. Substitute God for Godot. Our words, thoughts, and actions are devoid of meaning apart from the advent of God in Christ. And there, too, is the source of light—the light without which none of life makes sense.

Light arises out of darkness. Deliverance comes out of the dark, at times even amid despair. Out of the darkness of Israel's bondage in Egypt, Moses stepped forward. From within the blackness of the Babylonian exile, Isaiah began to minister. During the darkest days of the Roman Empire, Augustine appeared on the scene. In that historical period known as the Dark Ages, Thomas Aquinas labored. Penetrating the darkness of the American Civil War was the strong light of leadership emanating from a man named Lincoln. Light arises as a means of deliverance from darkness.

Light and deliverance are realistic hopes, no matter how dark the situation in which the hopes arise.

This is the message of Advent, so crucial as a part of the gospel. Advent begins with waiting, waiting in darkness. But make no mistake, that is not where Advent ends. Advent is a pilgrimage toward light. At the end of Advent is a brilliant deliverance.

From this message come three conclusions. Each is worthy of careful consideration as another Advent begins.

First, *God is in our waiting.* The Old Testament is an Advent book filled with stories of waiting. However, God is there, in the Old Testament, in the waiting. Old Testament writers dramatically describe the mighty acts of God. Some of the greatest messianic literature preserved in the Old Testament developed during the darkest periods of Israel's history.

In the New Testament as well, darkness and waiting are prevalent themes. There, too, both the darkness and the waiting were pervaded by God's presence. The strength of the Christian church has often been revealed most clearly during bleak periods of persecution and duress.

We embark upon Advent knowing full well that light has broken and Jesus has come. Yet waiting is still a part of our present. So is darkness. Both will be significant factors with which we must cope during our personal journeys through Advent this year. At times each may be so heavy, so demanding, that we almost lose sight of the truth of the season.

Allow what is in your head to move to your heart as well. Times of waiting are a part of the essence of life. Remember Samuel, Isaiah, Job, and other spiritual kin. When we are waiting, even when we are waiting in darkness, we are not alone. God is in our waiting.

A second truth to be discovered in the message of Advent is that *light is a gift.* Regardless of how much we want light, we cannot make it happen. We cannot stare at a blackened horizon until we force a ray of brightness. Light—true light—is a gift from God.

True, one tiny spark of light can dispel a mass of darkness, but we must wait for that spark. Light comes as a gift.

Throughout Advent our eyes are fixed on the horizon where heaven and earth meet. We stare at that space intently, eager to catch sight of the first glimmer of light—whether a brief flicker or a quickly widening ray. In this sense, Advent is the story of our lives. We are always waiting for light. We wait because we know that if light is ever to be experienced, it must be received as a gift.

Finally, keep in mind that *God can and will see us through the darkness and save us by light.* Promise becomes fulfillment. Anticipation gives way to awareness. Life can change. Darkness is transformed into light. Advent is a time for shouting these truths in such a manner that no one misses them.

Do not lose sight of what is at stake here. The Advent narratives are not just neat stories about a strange star shining over a Galilean hillside or a brilliant light hovering over a stable somewhere in Bethlehem. The message of Advent involves truth about darkness and light in our lives.

Those of us who have spent so much time waiting should prepare for a change. Light is coming. Light can come to our lives. Our sins can be forgiven as this light falls upon us. Lives can be saved as this light penetrates our lives and becomes our guide.

Light is coming—light that we can see, light that we can know, light that we can accept. While standing bathed in this light, we will be able to see even more light. We will have a vision of the Light who can save our lives and our world. Christlight!

The best way to begin an observance of Advent is to resolve to wait. Start the season by waiting. Once again, the light seeks to be reborn amid darkness. Wait and make ready. The light seeks to be born in us, to shine in us, to shine through us.

We have lived in darkness long enough. Watch now as the light breaks. Embrace it. Rejoice as the light shines. Accept the light into your life. Be done with darkness and live in the light. Christlight!

The Promise of Dawn

Isaiah 9:2-9

Awakening to the Light

Come with me now. By way of the words on these pages, journey with me to that splendid moment when light breaks. Be careful with your eyes. Very likely they have become accustomed to darkness. Though you cannot see anything, you can stare comfortably into blackness. That must change.

Suddenly, while peering into darkness; suddenly, as if you were privileged to stand alongside God in creation and hear the Divine command, "Let there be light"; suddenly, you see light—not much, just a little. It is in the distance, but you can see it. The blackness stretched across the horizon appears to be splitting apart, gloriously divided by light.

Instinctively, you begin rubbing your eyes as they adjust to light. At first, all you can discern is a very thin line of brightness. Then, incredibly, shafts of brilliant orange and rays of bright yellow mixed with streaks of gold, pink, and rose shoot out across the sky like rocketed fireworks. For a brief moment you only can gasp at the beauty before you. Quickly, you adjust your eyes again, refocus your vision, so as not to miss even the most minute part of the full spectacle, a total explosion of light.

Sunrise is near. Any second the huge blazing red sphere will lift above the horizon. Anticipation of that sight creates joy and excitement. Darkness is about to be totally dispelled. In just a moment the whole earth will be drenched in sunlight. Already the sky seems to be on fire with light, racing toward every shadowed corner of the land. All that remains to be seen is the sun itself, but it is not in view—yet.

Such is the situation during the second week of Advent. We are at dawn—only a fleeting second removed from total darkness, only a short breath away from sunrise. The description is physical, but the meaning is spiritual.

At stake here is not the arrival of a new day. The darkness under attack from the inbreaking light is composed of the shadows of our lives—the evil, the frustration, the depression, the despair. The light is God's presence. Christlight.

The sun is not up, but dawn is certain. Though we have not yet seen all there is to be seen, we are in the right place to see it, to see it all. Our vision is cast in the right direction. We wait with an excitement sustained by confidence. Soon still more light will appear.

Incidentally, we are in good company standing on this spot. Look around. Nearby is Isaiah, a prophet whose ministry amid darkness suddenly was flooded with light. Zechariah is also present, a priestly old man whose darkened hopes of ever fathering a child were completely surprised by the brilliance of a light-hearted birth announcement. Mary is here, too—the young woman whose darkness of unanswered questions gave way to her awareness of truth. Living at dawn, we are in very good company.

Isaiah wrote about life in this place. We will do well to read the words framed by this wise prophet as he awakened to light. Then, too, we can be helped by two magnificent outbursts—one from Zechariah when his and Elizabeth's son, John the Baptist, was born and the other from Mary who could not contain her joy over the prospect of being the mother of Jesus. Caught up in a similar moment in time, just after darkness has been dispelled and just before the full light of day has arrived, we are in an excellent position to learn from these people.

A little light has broken into our lives; however, we feel a desperate need for more. Life at dawn is life on the boundary—the boundary between a past not too distant and a future not quite present. At dawn, on the boundary—we hear God's Word on this stop in our pilgrimage through Advent.

Right off, we are captivated by a part of the message which speaks about...

Relief from Fear

Darkness feeds fear. Everybody knows that. A toothache hurts much worse during the long hours of a night than in the light of day. A storm in the evening is much more terrifying than a storm in the morning when the work of the wind can be seen. A strange sound in the night sets off a fear that never would arise in the light of day.

Light from God is a powerful antidote to fear. The prophet Isaiah found his hopes lifted by a promise of the coming of one who would alleviate all fear—the advent of one called "Wonderful Counselor, Mighty God, Eternal Father, Prince of Peace" (Isa. 9:6). When an angel of God appeared to Zechariah to announce the pregnancy of his wife Elizabeth, the angel's first words formed the admonition, "Don't be afraid, Zechariah!" (Luke 1:13, GNB). The heavenly messenger who spoke to Mary said reassuringly, "Don't be afraid, Mary" (v. 30, GNB). Nine months later, when Mary's pregnancy had gone full term and Jesus was born, the skies over Bethlehem were filled with a whole host of angels heralding the good news of Jesus' birth, and a group of startled shepherds was told, "Don't be afraid!" (2:10, GNB).

Relief from fear is a recurring theme in all of the biblical narratives related to Christ's birth. Light from God is a powerful antidote to fear. The message for people at dawn is, "Don't be afraid."

An old story, probably apocryphal, from the life of the founder of Christian monasticism communicates this truth. Supposedly Saint Anthony was being besieged by demons—all kinds of demons materializing in a variety of forms. Finally, after battling numerous reptiles and wild beasts, Saint Anthony collapsed to the floor groaning in pain. At that very moment, deliverance came. As the monk looked upward, the ceiling above him seemed to open up to allow a heavenly beam of light to shine directly upon him. That radiant light drove the demons from Saint Anthony's life and the pain from his body. Light! Divine light brings relief from human fears.

Imagine the possibility of relief from fear, the fears dominating your thoughts, increasing your anxieties, draining your energies even as you read these words. The thought seems almost too good to be true. But that is precisely the promise of the gospel. We may hear it best at dawn as pilgrims journeying through Advent, though the good news of relief from fear is for all times and for people everywhere.

There is more. Another dimension of the Advent truth about dawn constructs...

A Foundation for Hope

The ancient Hebrews considered dawn a sign from God that darkness would not last forever. Little wonder, then, that dawn was associated so closely with light. Words from the psalmist show us the intensity involved: "I wait for the Lord more eagerly than watchmen wait for the dawn" (130:6, GNB).

How badly dawn is needed! In our world and in our lives, we need some assurance that darkness—complete, threatening, killing darkness—never again will envelop us. Is that too much to ask?

No! Advent, particularly that part of Advent analogous to dawn, offers assurance about the vitality of hope. Christian hope is real, true. The promise to which it clings is certain to be fulfilled. Christian hope is not to be confused with escapist musings, with wishful thinking, or with fanciful daydreaming. (Christian hope is no magical phenomenon by which fulfillment of the personal desires of every believer can be guaranteed.) The hope heralded by Advent—Christian hope—is distinctive. Its foundation is solid, its outlook is realistic, and its implementation is sure. Such hope is enhanced by every experience of dawn. Already the long-awaited light is breaking. Life in total light is near.

Look again at the prophet Isaiah. His stirring comments about the birth of a baby of divine deliverance were followed by an avalanche of problems. Hard times arrived. Troubles mounted. Some people were even carted off into bondage in a strange land. Did Isaiah apologize for an optimism? Hardly. In the midst of trying difficulties, with his hope severely under siege, Isaiah wrote, "The people who walked in darkness have seen a great light" (9:2).

Notice that the tenses of his verbs indicate an accomplished fact. He doesn't say, "They will see light sometime later." He says, "They *have* seen a great light." Surrounded by darkness, Isaiah had no question whatsoever that hopes for light would be realized.

Such certainty is the substance of Advent-inspired hope. Christian hope is not a "pie in the sky by and by" type of opiate. Christian hope is a present reality. The future awaited—hoped for and prayed for—has now begun. We speak confidently of the fact that we will be saved because we know with certainty that in Christ we have been saved and through Christ we are being saved. Light is an important dimension of our hope for the future because light is a significant aspect of our experience in the past. It all happened at dawn, and at dawn it happens every time. Now, it is dawn.

Inevitably, God's actions will supersede our expectations. Our hope never will be big enough to capture what God has in store for us. We simply do not have the capacity to comprehend God's ways.

Isaiah envisioned a national king. God gave the whole world a Savior. The prophet longed for justice and peace made possible by the reign of a descendant of David. God made possible the establishment of justice among all people and peace between all nations by means of salvation through a Suffering Servant. The inability to perceive the fullness of divine glory is a component of the human condition. Thank God our hopes never will be large enough to contain God's plans or to define God's works.

As Advent pilgrims who have arrived at dawn, we now know that we do not have to live in fear and without hope. Never again does life have to be completely devoid of light. What more good possibly could be added to these realizations? Only an . . .

Invitation to Faith

Utilizing what probably was the text of an old baptismal hymn, the apostle Paul wrote, "the time has come for you to wake up from your sleep. For the moment when we will be saved is closer now than it was when we first believed. The night is nearly over, day is almost here. . . . Let us conduct ourselves properly, as people who live in the light of day" (Rom. 13:11-13, GNB). In that statement is the essence of the invitation extended to every individual as light breaks. We are summoned to faith, to live in the light—Christlight.

Yet most of our experiences occur along the boundary between darkness and light. Darkness—the dark side of life—still seems to be very much with us even as the light begins to break. Realistically, we can walk in either direction—chasing the shadows and seeking more darkness or sprinting toward the horizon, which is beginning to blaze with light. Standing there, rubbing our eyes while we try to adjust to light, we have to make a decision.

Christ is where the light is. In fact, Christ is the reason for the light. Christ invites everybody to live with Him in the light of faith—to allow His light to shine on people, in people, and through people. The divine invitation necessitates a human decision. We can walk toward Christ or we can walk away. The difference between the two is the difference between daylight and darkness.

Any hesitancy on our part to respond positively to this invitation may be the product of a confusion of traditions. Unfortunately, many people are much more familiar with the popular symbols of this season than with the realities to which these symbols point. Christmas lights are an example.

At this time of the year, everybody talks about the marvelous spirit which permeates people. Call it what you will—a positive outlook, a sense of goodwill, or, as some say, "Christmas cheer." What is felt inside is tied up with what is seen outside, especially with those little multicolored lights which are wrapped around trees, dangled from utility poles, displayed in store windows, and stretched across the rooflines of houses. The small electric lights are symbols inspired by the eternal saving Light. See the lights and catch the "Christmas spirit."

Christmas lights blink, sparkle, rotate, and radiate color as they shine. However, the bulbs which carry the light can be turned on and off at will. The brilliance of Christmas lights depends totally upon the whims of human action. Shortly after Christmas Day, by all means by the end of the calendar year, these colorful, delightful little bulbs are taken down and put in storage. Soon after, perhaps immediately, we sense that the warm feelings we enjoyed so much during Advent are now absent. We are back to business as usual. Our routines look like ruts. Days are short. Darkness comes quickly. What on earth has happened? Did "the good news of great joy" get mixed up with the decorative lights and shoved into storage, out of sight?

Don't let Christmas lights block your view of the Christlight of Advent. The Advent invitation to faith, the Advent summon to live in the light, is unlike even the brightest decorations of Christmas. Instead, we need to remember that God's coming among us in light and the invitation for us to join Jesus in light involve a totally unique light—a light that never goes out. Never!

Try to prevent dawn. Stop, if you can, one single shaft of that golden light which shoots across the early morning sky. You cannot do it. Nobody can stop that light. People can place blinders over their eyes and pull down shades to cover their windows. But they cannot stop the light.

Such is the power of the Advent invitation. Light is breaking—ready or not, like it or not. The Kingdom of Light is arriving. Jesus, whose birth gave rise to all of this light, whose very identity in adulthood was that of "the Light of the World," and whose birthday celebration is best understood as a festival of light, invites us to receive both Him and the light, and to live with Him in the light.

One of the first Christian missionaries to work among Muslim people claimed as his motto: "The Lord is my Light." The invitation of Advent challenges all people to make that missionary's motto a personal profession.

On November 1, 1918, the light of morning broke over the city of Mons. Many residents thought they would not live to see this day. All night long a dreary darkness had been penetrated only by sporadic flashes of gunfire. For four and a half years the citizens had lived in the darkness of war. But on this day, at dawn, the last of the enemy troops withdrew from the territory. News raced through the city like a wildfire. People streamed into the streets dancing and shouting in jubilation. Business people and house dwellers were told, "Hang out your flags." So at dawn on that November morning, as the light of a new day broke over the city of Mons, banners blew in the wind and people celebrated their newfound freedom in ecstatic joy. At long last, darkness was over. Peace had arrived with the light.

That historical event has a spiritual counterpart. Once more now, look—no, study—the moment when light breaks. Surely, you have been there before—everyone has been there, waiting for the light, hoping for the light, praying for the light. Receive with joy the Advent message for this moment. Old Isaiah first put us on to it, and the gospel writers have filled our souls with it: "Unto us a child is born." Unto us—a child, a dawn, a light—Christlight.

Wishful thinking and fantasizing aside, we can know relief from fear. Everyone has reason to acknowledge a strong foundation for hope. An invitation to faith can be accepted. From this time on, life can be lived in light.

Watch the horizon so you can see the light breaking. Right now, in this Advent season, we are just moments removed from darkness and only an instant away from sunrise, but we are in the light. Thanks be to God, we are in the light. Hang out the banners. Shout and sing of hope. Express faith in words and deeds. Celebrate the dawn. Live in the light—Christlight.

The Attraction of Sunrise

1 John 1:5-7; 2:7-11

Pursuing the Light

*T*he night seemed as long as it did strange. That morning I had preached in Texas. During the late afternoon I had flown to Miami. A colleague and I were going to Rio de Janeiro, Brazil, to be a part of a missions venture. We held reservations on a Miami to Rio flight scheduled to depart at midnight.

Time dragged in the Miami airport. The airline had overbooked a flight to Caracas, Venezuela. Three hundred people were talking excitedly about how to get to their destination. Airline officials were trying to decide whether to solve the problem by adding a flight or rerouting our flight through Caracas. Most of the words that filled the air were in a language I did not understand. Finally, a decision was made. Caracas passengers boarded another plane, and our flight departed.

By now my normal bedtime had long since passed, but the anticipation of new experiences and the excitement of the journey kept me alert. Eventually, the activities of the day took their toll. I remember watching the checkerboard of flickering lights as our plane climbed over the Florida coastline. Then I went to sleep.

My sleep was neither sound nor restful. The buckle of a fastened seat belt poked me uncomfortably. My legs were cramped. My neck was strained. But I did sleep. Several hours passed.

For some reason, probably to turn my head in search of a more restful position, I raised up a bit. As I shifted in my seat, I glanced out the window. Surprise! I was startled, absolutely stunned. Sunrise! Our flight was somewhere over the Atlantic

Ocean, and there was the sun, seeming to appear suddenly, a brilliant red sphere—relatively small at first, surrounded by an expanse of darkness that seemed to be running from it.

I wanted to go back to sleep. My eyes were more comfortable in darkness. But I had to look. The sun drew my attention like a magnet. I reached for my camera and snapped a picture, wanting to capture something of the magic of this moment forever. My eyes would not close. I could not make myself pull down the window shade. With each passing second, the light outside became brighter and brighter.

Soon the pilot of our aircraft announced that we were in our final approach above Rio de Janeiro. Hills covered with brilliant green foliage protruded through the puffy white clouds that hovered over the airport. I took a long deep breath as the wheels of our plane touched the ground in South America. A new day had been born.

Sunrise always brings a special set of joys:

How long I have waited for a reunion with my family. Today is the day. The sun is up.

A trip of a lifetime has been on the calendar for two years. Today we depart. I can hardly believe it. The time has arrived. Look at the sun breaking through the clouds.

The final exam is today. I think I am ready. I want to be finished with this course. I have studied all night. It's daylight.

Who wants to escape the promise of light or to shut out the substance of brilliance? The light—the sunrise—is bringing fulfillment and offering hope. Everybody wants to stay with it, to keep looking at it, and to pursue it so as to live in the light.

In the Bible this very commonplace, natural experience of sunrise becomes a way of describing the unique, saving experience of an encounter with God. Christ Himself created the analogy. The One who came as light talked about His coming in terms of light. In 1 John, the writer says, "This is the message we have heard from him"—and there is no mistaking the fact that "Him" means Jesus. "God is light" (1:5). John conveys a word to us that comes straight from Christ.

That biblical analogy is the background of the use and symbolism of lights during Advent. Jesus spoke of His life as light.

And He talked of the possibility of life in Him in terms of light.

By next week, we will be so close to Christmas that we can hardly think of anything other than the story of Jesus' birth as told by Luke. Before we get there, though, glance back. This worship-oriented journey through Advent began with thoughts about waiting for the light. Exploring the dilemma of darkness, we discovered that God is in our waiting. Then we rubbed our eyes and adjusted our sight to the inbreaking light of dawn. Good news abounded: fear can be set aside, hope grasped, and faith experienced. We knew we were well on our way to Christmas. Now we are close. Probably, at this point in Advent, most of us would just as soon skip over the intervening days and get on with Christmas Day. However, the emphasis of this week is critical. We miss it to the detriment of our spiritual pilgrimage.

The symbolism of light and darkness hints at a mysticism that makes many people uncomfortable. The celebration of Christ's birth seems like only a romantic interlude in a rough-and-tumble world. Would mature people really travel to bow down before a whimpering baby lying in an out-of-the-way manger? Our hunch is no. But we go along with it all, not wanting to break the seasonal trance, hoping to contribute to a magical moment. For many people, moving to Christmas is like going to Disney World and finally seeing Cinderella's castle.

In 1 John, the author saves us from such wrongheaded thinking. John provides an insight about light that is practical, not mystical; realistic, not fanciful. His text tells us what it means to pursue light. Before rushing on to Christmas, we will do well to ponder John's narrative. With those truths in mind, time should be devoted to studying the true meaning of the incarnation and looking carefully at the total cost of an authentic celebration of it.

What does it mean to pursue light—the light of Christmas, Christlight? John provides several specific answers to that important question. Pursuing the light means...

Seeing Ourselves

False religion is a primary source of self-deception. We can fool ourselves so easily that the tendency is as common as it is dangerous. In the opening chapter of 1 John, the writer lists three elements of self-deception in people devoid of a relationship with God. He skillfully places their claims in an ascending order of severity: "We have fellowship with him" (1:6), "We have no sin" (v. 8), and "We have not sinned" (v. 10).

Standing in the light of God's presence, we see as we have never seen before. Nothing looks as different as ourselves. Stripped of our masks, without the enhancement of spiritual cosmetics, unable to speak a deceptive word, illumined by Christlight, we see ourselves as we are. Like it or not, ready or not, we have to admit weaknesses, acknowledge needs, and confess sins.

Such a situation of honesty and vulnerability can be terrifying. We may not like what we see. Discouragement and guilt can develop. However, pursuing the light also involves...

Experiencing Forgiveness

Fellowship with God is impossible apart from forgiveness for our sins. That means divine pardon for our rebellion against God. Pursuing the light—Christlight—involves seeking forgiveness. However, the object of our search is precisely the substance of God's gift. Forgiveness! God wants to extend forgiveness to us as much as we need to seek forgiveness from God.

Celebrations of Christmas make little sense without confessions of sin on our part and a reception of divine forgiveness. This is what daylight is all about.

If we refuse to acknowledge our personal need for God, refrain from any confession of sin, and deny our need for forgiveness, we will do best to stay away from the manger and take a place with the crowds around the cross. An unrepentant posture is much more appropriate in relation to the crucifixion of Jesus than to a celebration of His birth. Receiving Christ, pursuing His light, means experiencing forgiveness.

Also involved in a pursuit of Christlight is...

Doing the Truth

Though most everybody recognizes the crucial importance of truth in a pursuit of light, not everyone sees that truth involves action as well as speech. Even some translations of the Bible fail to capture this insight from John. Pursuing the light means "doing" the truth. Integrity is a matter of *deeds* as well as words. Integrity is a mark of the life-style of one who follows Christlight.

Sometime back, I came across the term "Discussion Group Christianity." What a misleading phrase! Truth is not a body of information to be studied and talked about. Neither is Christianity. Truth is to be lived. So is Christianity.

Bible study is important, but Bible study can become a diversion from the Christian life unless the truths that are studied are also practiced. Issues-oriented discussions can degenerate into a sophisticated form of pseudofaith unless the truth affirmed in words becomes the truth incarnated in behavior.

The imagery in 1 John is important. Christianity is best understood by means of verbs—walking in the light, *doing* the truth. The best celebrations of Christ's birth are action-filled demonstrations of the truth of Christ's life.

A resolve to *do* the truth results in a recognition that another important dimension of pursuing the light is...

Living Morally

On one occasion, a British statesman named Lord Morley traveled from England to a Canadian university to deliver a series of lectures. After making his way to the rostrum for his first address, Morley reportedly said, "I have traveled four thousand miles to tell you that there is a difference between right and wrong."

Talking about morality during Advent may provoke restlessness if not resentment among some people. "Wait. Hold it right there. Let's get back to the Galilean hillsides and angels singing in the sky. Don't burden us with reminders about honesty in business dealings, purity in personal lifestyles, and peace among nations. We hear enough of that stuff already. We need to celebrate Christ's birth."

What does Christ's birth, the arrival of Christlight, have to do with the way I treat my family, how I feel about nuclear arms, what I do about hunger, the materials I read, the way I talk, and the manner in which I spend my money? The answer to these questions is "Everything!" Christlight has everything to do with everything. No area of life is off-limits to the redemptive, transforming light of Christ's presence.

Here is Christmas without tinsel, but it is just as much an expression of the season as anything that glitters. Christ's birth is celebrated when Christ's followers live morally day in and day out.

John leaves no room for misunderstanding about this matter. He writes that a person who claims fellowship with Christ, yet continues to walk in darkness, lies. If people say they are ready for Christmas and continue to walk in darkness (live as if Christ had not come), they lie. To fall before the manger in adoration yet ignore the demands of Christ is more than hypocrisy. It is blatant dishonesty. Pursuing the light means living morally.

John declares as well that pursuing the light involves...

Abiding in Love

In 1 John, the writer relates hatred to darkness and love to light. Christ, the light, is the incarnation of love. Receiving Christ means living in love and with love. True pilgrims in pursuit of the light learn to love even the seemingly unlovable.

Love is an overused word. Aldous Huxley expressed my sentiments exactly when he said, "Of all the worn, smudged, dog-eared words in our vocabulary, 'love' is certainly the grubbiest, smelliest, slimiest. Bawled from a million pulpits, lasciviously crooned through hundreds of millions of loudspeakers, it has become an outrage to good taste and decent feeling, an obscenity which one hesitates to pronounce. And yet, it has to be pronounced, for, after all, Love is the last word."[9]

Jesus defines love best. To live in fellowship with Jesus is to live in the light. And to live in the light is to live in love. A brief text from the ancient *Testament of Levi* states this truth superbly:

> Lighting up the light of knowledge
> as the sun the day...
> He shall shine forth as the sun
> on the earth...
> And there shall be peace in
> all the earth.

After a lifetime of studying and writing history, Will Durant distilled his work into three words: "Love one another." The great philosopher acknowledged that his conclusion coincided with the essence of Jesus' teaching. To those who would scoff at his words, Durant offered the recommendation that love be tried. He declared that, in his opinion, love is the most practical thing in the world.[10]

Celebrating Christmas, pursuing the light, includes reconciliation with God and more. Walking in Christlight means becoming reconciled with other people and with them abiding together in love.

One other insight from 1 John is worthy of mention. According to this New Testament author, pursuing the light means...

Sharing with Others

How do we know about Christmas? Why do we identify the coming of Christ with the arrival of light and the heralding of good news? The answer to both questions is the same. And simple. Someone told us. Someone told us about Christmas and its meaning. Someone told us about Christ and His meaning.

John proclaimed for others what he had been told by others and what he had experienced for himself. Discovering light then not sharing it does not make sense. Such inaction is as unthinkable as receiving a wonderful Christmas gift and not wanting to tell someone else about it.

Not only is keeping the good news of Christmas to oneself unthinkable, it is sinful. To accept Christ's coming without sharing in the telling of that event is pure self-centeredness. The light is not for us alone. The light of Christ is for all people who walk in darkness. All who pursue the light, preparing themselves to receive and celebrate its rising, are to live as children of light, by which the lives of others are illumined.

A great old hymn, appropriate for Advent, sets people to singing about the necessity of sharing the good news of Christ with others.

> O Zion, haste, thy mission, high fulfilling,
> To tell to all the world that God is Light;

That He who made all nations is not willing
One soul should perish, lost in shades of night.[11]

The refrain to this musical piece is a welcome missionary mandate to followers of Christ, to children of light. All are encouraged to seize a joyful, fulfilling opportunity:

Publish glad tidings, tidings of peace,
Tidings of Jesus, redemption and release.[12]

To pursue the light of Christ is a practical not a mystical endeavor. From the writer of 1 John come six specific suggestions about practical ways to pursue Christ's light and celebrate Christ's birth. We are to see ourselves, experience forgiveness, do the truth, live morally, abide in love, and share with others. How could the content of our Advent journey to Christmas be any clearer?

Already the light is breaking. The sun is rising. No wonder we are attracted to it. To discover the light is to find Christ. To know Christ is to experience salvation. And to have salvation is to be able to say, "I see!"

How can anyone not be attracted to a sunrise? Why would anyone hesitate to pursue Christlight? Refusing to live in the light of Christ is like denying sunshine. It is like standing in rays of warm, healing sunlight and declaring, "I believe it is best to walk in the chill and danger of darkness."

Central to Advent is the announcement, "Welcome to the light!" Light—not just any light, but *the* light—is available to all people. Light is everywhere. We can see where we are going—not only on our way to Christmas but on our journey into all of the future.

Advent is the time to resolve to live in the light, and to make a covenant with God to share with others the light which we enjoy so much for ourselves. We can celebrate the light seasonally. It's time for that. But we can also begin a walk in the light that will last forever. Surely, it's time for that as well.

Welcome to the light. Christlight!

The Joy of Day

Luke 2:8-15; John 1:4-5, 9

Celebrating the Light

*I*magine that you are standing in the woods in darkness—total darkness. No streetlights. No lights from passing cars. No yard lights. Darkness. Your eyes have adjusted to a lack of light. Still, all you can see is blackness. You would like to move, but you do not dare. You do not know where to step or how to step. Good judgment overrides desire as you decide it is best to stay where you are and wait for light.

Suddenly lightning flashes. Instantly, the black sky is gone. The world seems drenched with brightness. You can see a series of steps in front of you, a walkway that leads to safety. Light is everywhere, light as bright as the sky at midday. Your heart skips a beat in excitement. Your spirit seems ready to soar. Then, just as suddenly, the light is gone. Impenetrable darkness returns.

Such a situation is an apt analogy for Christmas, with one major exception. At Christmas, the light that dispels the darkness remains. Against the light of Christ, darkness does not have a prayer.

Darkness was suddenly shattered by the birth of the Savior. Light! "The Word became flesh" (John 1:14). Light flooded the earth, spilling across all barriers and dispelling shadows. The all-encompassing brilliance was no passing phenomenon. "The true light...was coming into the world" (v. 9). Darkness was doomed. Christlight was here to stay.

Years later John wrote, "The light shines in the darkness and the darkness has not overcome it" (v. 5). At the time of Christ's birth, the angel offered the best description of what happened, "For to you is born this day in the city of David a Savior who is Christ the Lord" (Luke 2:11).

Through the ages, human words of response to God's Word in Christ have sought to match the majesty of the event—the moment, the message, the baby, the man. A primitive Christian hymn entitled *Phos hilaron* hails Jesus as

> Serene light of the Heavenly Glory
> Of the Father Everlasting.[13]

An early Christian creed confesses Christ as "Light of Light." In the opening to his third book of *Paradise Lost,* John Milton writes, "Hail, holy light! Offspring of heav'ns first born."[14] Many older editions of church hymnals contain the beautiful text of "Light of the World, We Hail Thee."

> Light of the world, we hail Thee,
> Flushing the eastern skies;
> Never shall darkness veil Thee
> Again from human eyes.[15]

But wait! Hold on! All of that is poetry. That is not where we live. Poets are not a part of our world. What we know best is the stark, straightforward prose of *The Wall Street Journal* or a local newswriter. No one likes to throw cold water on a celebration, but before this "light" theme gets out of hand, some nagging questions have to be answered. Is the nativity of Christmas a mere Currier and Ives setup? Must all who speak of Christmas sound like the writers for greeting cards? What does it mean to welcome in-breaking light? Get specific. What is the news of great joy? Babies are born every day. What is different here? Why the angels? Why the worship? Why the poetry and music about light?

If you think such inquiries impertinent, think again. These questions direct our thoughts to the substance at the center of the celebration called Christmas. Is everyone to be happy just because it is December and a time for festivity? If not, why? What is the meaning of this birth that is described often in language of light?

What is unique about the baby involved? What are we celebrating? And why?

The Bible answers those questions. Each is best understood as it becomes personal. We celebrate the light of Christ's birth because...

God Is Revealed

The renowned New Testament scholar W. D. Davies describes Jesus as the "exegesis of God." Jesus shows us what God is like. The person of Christ is God in human form. Jesus reveals God.

Because Christ came, we are able to know something of the depth of God's compassion, the extent of God's justice, the bounty of God's grace, and the possibility of God's gift of peace. Look at Jesus and truth is illumined. God loved the creation so much that God chose to dwell in it. The evidence is in Bethlehem. God so desires fellowship with all people that God took action to assure salvation for every person who will receive it. The great, Almighty God of creation, the mighty God who brought everything into being by a simple command, came into this world on the back side of a Middle Eastern village and was laid in a manger.

I must confess that questions still hound me at times. *How easy it must be for God to prescribe life for us when God does not have to face the difficulties of life among us,* I think. *How would God fare if God had to live as we do?* I wonder. *Could God stick to lofty Commandments if God had to dwell in some of the dingy valleys in which we have to walk?* I speculate. *Could God actually love enemies that had to be encountered daily up close rather than theorized about within some mystical, eternal sphere?* I ask myself. Jesus responds to my thoughts and answers my questions before I can put words around my ideas. Jesus answers not with abstractions but in the incarnation. God is revealed in Christ. Jesus provides concrete (fleshed-out) evidence of how God would live in this world.

Christlight is not a distant glow, the brilliance of a bygone day. The light emanating from Jesus' birth is for the present. Bethlehem was by no means the last stage on which God's drama of redemption would be enacted. Words from the psalmist are applicable to Jesus: "Because of your light, we see the light" (Ps. 36:9, GNB). Just when we think we are alone in a silent, dark, God-forsaken world, Christ opens our eyes to what God is presently doing among us and to what God lovingly wants to do with us.

We celebrate the light because in it (Him) God is revealed and by it (Him)...

Dread Is Defeated

John seems to have chosen his words carefully. The author of the fourth Gospel describes Jesus as "the real light" (1:9, GNB). That is to say, Jesus is authentic. You can count on this light. Every claim about it is true.

Many people dread the truth. They have been fooled, disappointed, and disillusioned too often. They fear that discovering the truth will be disturbing and depressing. Somebody always seems to have an answer to every question and a solution that will end all problems. The remedy seems simple—an easy diet by which one can eat all the food desired and still lose weight, a quick way to get rich momentarily, or a sure-fire method of gaining power over other people's lives. The world is full of simple steps to salvation. But now we know better. We tried the miracle diet and did not shed a pound. We read the fabulous book and did not add enough money to our income to pay for the book. We polished our sales pitch, and our rate of success was unaltered. We do not want any more disappointments. We dread huckster saviors and their promises of quick and easy salvation.

Hear the angel. "Fear not!" was the message from the skies over Bethlehem. And you can believe it. Everybody can count on the One whose birth set the angels to singing. No one needs to dread the truth in relation to Jesus. In fact, with Jesus, no one has to fear anything—*anything!* New Testament writers see that in relation to Jesus even death—the ultimate in big scares—has been robbed of its power to provoke fear.

No wonder a celebration breaks out around Jesus' birth. In Christlight, God is revealed, dread is defeated, and...

Guidance Is Offered

How should I live? What should I do? Can you tell me something that will help me get through the week? People flock to seminars with "how-to" titles: How to Succeed in Business, How to Find Happiness, How to Raise Healthy Children, How to Overcome Worry, How to Win Friends, How to Prepare for Retirement, How to Choose the Best "How-to" Seminar.

Professional advice abounds, and it is expensive. Answers are available for everyone seeking guidance about anything. Then, there is *the* answer, what John calls "the real light."

The Christ who came to our world shines His light on our lives, questions and all. Jesus is light, *the* Light, light to illumine our paths, light to expose our needs, light to reveal truth, light to lay bare our values, light to eradicate darkness, light to warm us, light to comfort us, light to attract us. Jesus Christ is light.

Christ's light is available as a guide for all people. In relation to Christ, all other means of guidance appear as little flashlights with weak batteries held against the never-ending brilliance of the sun.

A celebration of Christlight is in order. Guidance is offered and . . .

A Relationship Is Extended

Make no mistake about the message that stands at the end of Advent and the beginning of Christmas. All of this talk about darkness and light is not a seasonal foray into theories about symbols, myths, and abstractions. At the center of it all is a person. Jesus is here. Jesus is Emmanuel—"God with us." The light is a life. We are called into a relationship, a personal relationship. We can become children of light by giving ourselves to the One Who is every bit as much love as light. Walking in the light means more than following Jesus. It involves walking with Jesus and enjoying having Jesus walk with us.

In the gospel of Advent according to John, light and life go together. The two are inseparable. The light of Christ allows us to see the giver of life and leads us into a fullness of life. What is involved is extremely personal in nature. Celebrating light and receiving life go together. Each relates to a person's response to the light which comes from Bethlehem, the baby named Jesus.

This personal nature of the saving light is captured in a hymn text by Harriet Beecher Stowe:

> Still, still, with Thee, when purple morning breaketh,
> When the bird waketh, and shadows flee;
> Fairer than morning lovelier than daylight
> Dawns the sweet consciousness I am with Thee.[16]

Celebrating the light involves living in a relationship. The joy of Christmas is found not by looking to the heavens to catch a glimpse of a beam of light but by receiving into our hearts the person of light.

A final reason for rejoicing in the light is that in Christ...

History Is Fulfilled

Advent warns us not to make Christmas too small. Christmas is neither an individual nor a national celebration. The event which gave rise to the festival—the birth of Christ—is of cosmic proportions. It marks the high point of human history and instills that history with purpose and the promise of fulfillment. Our celebrations of Christmas should complement its largeness.

The good news of Christ's birth is a statement about our world and its history, as well as about God. This world is the place where God wants us to live. Fidelity to God does not require escape from the world. Not at all. God desires for people to live purposefully in the world. Admittedly, that is not easy, but we are not left to get by on our own. God has joined us in the world. "The Word became flesh and dwelt among us" (John 1:14). Subsequently, all of history, like all of creation, moves toward redemption.

Do you see?

That is a wonderful question for the fourth week of Advent. After spending nearly a month looking for light, do you see? Seeing is what the light is all about. Seeing is salvation.

Do you see the reasons for celebrating the light? Begin the drumrolls. Sound the trumpets. Shout the good news. God is revealed! Dread is defeated! Guidance is offered! Relationship is extended! History is fulfilled! Do you see? The time has come for the celebration of light to begin.

The joy of day can be experienced most fully as our lives are given to Christ completely. Commitment is the best form of celebration—a commitment to Christ.

An old story from a war zone tells of an aircraft carrier sailing the South Pacific in dangerously turbulent waters. As night came, one airplane was still searching for the ship. Enemy submarines were in the area, and lights were forbidden. Only the captain of the ship could give an order for light. He did. "Light up the ship!" The command rang out. At a terrific risk, the lights of the ship came on. The airplane was saved.[17]

In like manner, Christ came. The birth at Bethlehem was an obedient response to God's command, "Light up the world!" Here, too, were risks—the risk of ridicule, the risk of rejection, even the risk of crucifixion. But Christ came. The light shone in the darkness. And, as a result, people can be saved. People can live in the light.

Advent announces, "Now the light shines—Christlight!" We can turn our backs on the light and be judged by it. Or we can face the light, walk toward it, receive it, live in it, see, and experience salvation. Our response may be in question, but there is no doubt about the light. Christ's light shines. We cannot stop it, stamp it out, cover it up, or contain it. The world is flooded by it. We are bathed in it.

Legend has it that somewhere in the islands of the South Sea a monument stands to a faithful missionary. The inscription placed there to honor that noble gentleman captures precisely the essential commentary regarding Christ: "When he came, there was no light. When he left, there was no darkness."

So how should Advent conclude? Wake up, arise, skip, run, sing, and respond. The Word has become flesh. The Savior has been born. A great light is shining on the people who have been walking in darkness. The Savior is for us. The light shines on us. The Savior is with us.

The night is over. Day has come. Christ is here. Thanks be to God. Hallelujah! The light shines—Christlight!

PART IV

THE PRAYERS OF ADVENT

"O Come, O Come Emmanuel"

A Troubled Prayer

Isaiah 63:15; 64:1-12; 65:24

The Hope of Advent

*E*nvision a scene. Most likely it will not strike you as an appropriate backdrop against which to begin the journey of Advent. See it first, though, then decide.

A city is in ruins. Jerusalem has been destroyed. Once-mighty Israel has been reduced to a remnant. Scars from captivity cut deeply into the nation's psyche. Individuals feel the pain of bondage in their hearts. Windblown debris covers the ground where the temple formerly stood.

People are in the picture. However, none of them seems as somber as would be expected given the ravages of war all around them. An explanation becomes apparent. Casual conversations indicate that most of the individuals in the picture know little about the temple that once stood in great splendor. Surprisingly, they know still less about the God who previously was worshiped as Sovereign.

Things do not seem to be going well. Enemies of God greatly outnumber friends of God. Even if we count the weakest friends.

That is the scene.

Now, hear a voice. Pathos is in the voice, as are compassion, anger, anxiety, pleas, and mandates. A prophet is praying.

The prophet's prayer is a troubled petition. Yet the longer you listen to the prayer, the more certain you become that underlying all the problems that plague this man's life is a foundation of hope. It may be thin, but it is there. Slowly, you begin to sense as well that the troubled words of this prophet sound very much like a prayer appropriate for Advent, a prayer that you or I would pray.

Trouble. Hope. Advent. A strange mixture? Not really. Look.

The prophet feels alone. He has concluded that even God is distant and apathetic. Read his words: "Lord, look upon us from heaven, where you live in your holiness and glory. Where is your great concern for us? Where is your power? Where are your love and compassion? Do not ignore us" (Isa. 63:15, GNB).

A vivid awareness of the past creates nostalgia in the prophet and contributes to the urgency of his prayer. He is aware of many of God's dramatic visitations in days gone by. What he does not know firsthand, he has been told or he has read about. A cloud by day and a pillar of fire by night while Israel was in the wilderness. And who could ever forget the thunder and fire of Sinai! *Oh, if it could just be like that again,* the prophet must think. *Back then people believed in God, respected divine power, and welcomed holy compassion. If it could only be that way again!*

In his better moments, the prophet realizes that the troubles of the present are those that people have brought on themselves. Spiritual degeneracy has reached an all-time low as individuals blame their sins on God. No one prays much anymore or requests God's help. The prophet knows the truth. People have broken their covenant with God. They have built barriers to God's presence. They prefer darkness to light. Individuals bent on having their own way have created a chasm between themselves and God.

Almost overwhelmed by the situation, the prophet is moved to confession. Words spill out of his mouth painfully, "All of us have been sinful, even our best actions are filthy through and through" (64:6, GNB). The situation appears hopeless. Nothing can be done except ask God for mercy.

As this man of God prays, pouring out his troubles before God, his voice rises and falls. Suddenly the prophet cries out to God: "Why don't you tear the sky open and come down?... Come and reveal your power to your enemies and make the nations tremble at your presence!" (vv. 1-2, GNB).

The prophet wants a new day, longs for a radically different kind of future. He has had his fill of victories for evil, a proliferation of enemies, and the sovereignty of sin. In an impassioned plea, he implores God to appear. Let there be Advent! This man is ready for thunder and lightning in the skies, fire on the mountains, and fear among people. Enough is enough. It is time for God to show up, to get involved. The prophet concludes his prayer saying, "Lord are you unmoved by all this? Are you going to do nothing?" (v. 12, GNB) The last word of the prayer is followed by silence.

Wait a minute, you may be thinking, *where is any hope in all of that? Trouble is obvious. But how does all of this trouble point to even a speck of hope? We do not need trouble. We are beginning Advent. Why set bad news before us at this time of year?*

Study the situation carefully. The prophet was praying—*praying* not cursing—praying to God, praying with an expectation of response. In the past, the prophet had known God as Father and Redeemer. In fact, he continues to address God as both "Father" and "Redeemer." This man had not given up on God's sovereignty. At times sin may hide God's sovereignty, but sin cannot destroy it. The source of the trouble disturbing the prophet resides in the people of God, not in God. So a deeply disturbed prophet prays to God with a surprising amount of confidence. As a result, his confession paves the way for divine forgiveness and prepares him for God's appearance.

This prophet expects God's personal involvement with people. Though his prayer contains a request for the advent of the messianic age, the prophet's piercing cry conveys a plea for God's revelation through fire, not a person. This man wants an indication of the continuing reality of divine justice and compassion, but he does not imagine incarnation.

The weave of this Advent prayer consists of problems and promises, troubles and hope. Such is the tapestry of most Advent prayers.

Advent begins. Honestly, our minds are barely off Thanksgiving. Practically everybody talks of how badly we need Christmas. Most people admit, though, that they are not ready for Christmas and not particularly ready to start getting ready. Nevertheless, we want Christmas to come again. No one wants a year without Christmas.

Reading Isaiah's prayer is eerie. His words could be our words. Some of them are. He voiced many of the feelings that we experience as we turn our faces toward Bethlehem. From all we have read and been told, we sense that God was much more active in the past than in the present, certainly more dramatic in appearance. We have heard how our predecessors reverenced God. Now people are not interested in the church; they are preoccupied with themselves. God is barely acknowledged, much less served.

Many of the folks who seek to be most faithful to God, who are tired of battling great difficulties encountered while trying to do good and weary of harassment from their peers, want another dramatic intrusion by the divine. We say a loud "Amen" to the prophet's cry to God, "Why don't you tear the sky open and come down?" We want an advent with all the trappings. We want God to appear in such a manner as to strike fear in the people who have troubled us and to vindicate our exemplary lives. We would like to mount a soapbox against a backdrop of divinely ignited fireworks and declare to the rest of the world, "We told you so." Right or wrong, we want judgment over grace. At least that is the way we feel as we begin to pray.

We, too, want a new future. Everybody longs for a future without disease, worry, and conflict. Few, though, would argue that we *deserve* that kind of future. The world is pretty much as we have made it. We wanted to be on our own, and so we wrote God out of our lives. Now we know that was wrong. We need God. We want God to come back, to enter our lives again—stage right, stage left, or center stage, it does not matter; maybe with a loud bang, if that is not asking too much.

Our technology has outdistanced our morality. Today we can rebel against God more comprehensively, more efficiently, and with greater sophistication than ever before. Our efforts to destroy each other can be accompanied by state-of-the-art weaponry.

A sense of vocation has given way to a resolve to wheel and deal in business. Making money is now more important than experiencing personal fulfillment. Religious involvements have become more and more traditional and institutional and less and less personal. The church is just another nonprofit, civic organization, a good hedge just in case there really is a God.

We want a new future. We need Advent. What are we to do? What can we do? The ancient prophet points the way. All we can do is ask for God's mercy.

But *we can ask!* There. That is the hope of Advent. It always has been. We can ask for God's mercy.

Most Advent prayers take form amid troubled people. Who is not troubled in some way? Trouble, though, does not silence prayers or negate faith. Our belief in a compassionate God may be beleaguered, but it is still intact. The first words that form in our minds and pass across our lips are "Our Father." Our *Father*. The way in which we address God says it all. Our words reveal our most profound hope.

The truth to be pondered during Advent is that God has come to this troubled world. God appeared in thunder and lightning, but God also has been seen in a person, in a baby at Bethlehem. God comes to us, to each of us, where we live. The God who comes to us knows us and loves us anyway. This God takes on our hurts and joins our journeys through difficult times. The God revealed in Jesus Christ desires to come into our hearts.

Praying to God for help is a most appropriate way to begin the Advent pilgrimage. Requesting that God show up in our midst gets right to the heart of the season. The God who came will come again and again.

God hears the troubled prayer of a person who is not ready for Advent but longs for Christmas. In the case of the Old Testament prophet, a troubled person's prayer was answered. Isaiah wrote down God's response, "Even before they finish praying to me, I will answer their prayers" (Isa. 65:24, GNB). God hears us. God knows our troubles. God will help. We may have to wait a bit for God to act, but we will not have to wait long.

And when God acts, all may not go as we have expected. The prophet wanted a mountaintop experience with God that would cause the whole world to rise up and take notice. However, God slipped into the universe almost unnoticed, taking up residence where animals were sheltered and fed. People wanted the messianic age to be ushered in by a series of eye-catching, heart-stopping, divine disclosures. The Messiah appeared first as a helpless baby. Even on the night of nights, trouble and hope existed side by side.

Trouble does not negate hope. Not then. Not today. Our problems with darkness cannot snuff out our vision of light. So as the Advent journey begins again, we will do well to speak honestly of our needs to God. Talk of trouble will not drive the Christ away. Rather, it will encourage His coming. We will do well to confess our sins to God; Christ comes as the author of forgiveness. We will do well to affirm our hope before God. Our hope is an invitation for Jesus to come among us.

Of course, we must admit that our track record is not too good when God has been among us. Actually, we have not always treated God even with respect, much less obedience. The words of the old spiritual "Sweet Little Jesus Boy"[18] come very close to a precise description of our past. We didn't know who Jesus was.

But we are not prisoners of that past. We can do better. This time, this year, things are going to change for the good.

Not all people pray alike. The spirit of a prayer varies from person to person. However, the content of most prayers is remarkably the same. One individual, ready to throw her hands into the air and say, "I quit," instead quietly sighs, "Come, Lord Jesus." Another person, prays, "Come, Messiah, come." Still other people, weary in their struggles but determined not to quit, forcefully implore God, "Come, be with us, Lord." Some, how many is hard to say, cry out with impatience and desperation, "Come, Lord! Wilt thou keep silent forever?"

Not all people pray alike. But we all pray, somehow. Someway. We pray knowing that trouble, though we do not like it, may be the context in which hope is born. So we pray, acknowledging troubles and affirming hope. Throughout Advent, we pray for a new advent of God, and we pray with the certainty that God hears us and answers.

O come, O come, Emmanuel.

An Unanswered Prayer

Job 9:32-33

The Blessing of Advent

*J*ob does not look like a typical Advent worshiper. Neither does he sound like nor behave like one. However, Job's occasional outbursts to God are unmistakably prayers for Advent. One of Job's prayers in particular (the text of it is found in the Old Testament book that bears his name [9:32-33]) merits attention during the second week of this season.

None of the traditional Advent pageantry is present. No music, banners, greenery, angels, or star. No beauty of any kind. Job is in a ditch. Physically, emotionally, and spiritually, Job is in a ditch. Job speaks from a pit filled with refuse, a garbage dump. A most unlikely setting for an Advent drama.

Job is at the lowest point in his life. His body is covered by boils, infected by the pieces of broken pottery with which he has scraped them. His possessions have been destroyed. His children are dead. His heart is filled with grief. Even the three friends who came to visit Job tormented him more than they comforted him. Each seemed more interested in establishing his particular point of view than in offering consolation. Job is in a ditch.

Worse still is Job's relentless dissatisfaction with God. A person of faith can stand almost anything as long as there is an assurance of God's loving presence. Take that away, and even small burdens become unbearable. Job is not distraught because of God's apparent involvement in the calamities that have visited him and his family. Job is upset because of God's apparent refusal to vindicate his righteousness. In Job's mind all is lost. He is without property, children, friends, a good reputation, and God.

Amazingly, Job retains his faith in God even while he questions the actions of God. Job believes God to be kind and righteous. Sure, Job has doubts. In his shoes, who would be any different? Besides, the only way to avoid doubt completely is never to have serious thoughts. As certainly as anyone starts trying to understand God, God's ways, and the nature of a relationship with God, doubts come.

Job believes in God, and Job believes in himself. The source of his doubts is God's silence. Job wants to be vindicated. He longs for God to indicate in some fashion that he is a morally upright person. Under seige, bankrupt because of tragedy, and beleaguered by three hypocritical friends, Job wants God to write in the sky or to thunder throughout the universe, "Job is OK!"

Job is ready to give up. He has decided that he will not be proven righteous and just. That would require an act of God and obviously God is not going to appear. Job senses that he sits on the edge of an unbridgeable chasm. God is on the other side. The righteous God and Job, the righteous servant of God, seem hopelessly separated.

The situation appears bizarre, even extreme. Actually, it is a rather common phenomenon in human experience. Job is not the only person to feel deserted by God.

A young woman sits in my office speaking of her faith. Then she describes a bad situation in her family. She talks of sensing a broad expanse of separation from God. She cannot understand. Her belief is strong. Why does God not respond to her requests for help?

A businessman explains that, up to this point in his life, all of his professional pursuits have been guided by his understanding of God's leadership. Suddenly, everything has begun to go wrong. His career is coming apart. He still believes in doing God's will and wants to embody integrity, but he feels deserted. Why does God allow a devoted, obedient follower to get into such a bad predicament?

"Try to do right in this world and you will get clobbered!" A young CEO argues that the better he learns the secrets of success the more convinced he is that people who try to operate by ethics lose the big accounts. A mother admits her reservations about knowing how to counsel her children. She wants them to be good, but she does not want other people to take advantage of them. She is not sure she can have it both ways.

A teenager is bitter and bewildered. An athletic scholarship has been promised. Years of disciplined preparation are about to pay off. Then an injury occurs. Dreams are shattered. I listen to the young man, "Why? Why me? Why now? Where is our good, just, righteous God that takes care of people who try to do right? How could God create a universe in which such misfortune—no, injustice!—happens?"

Job has no idea of what can be done about his situation. He is in a pit, and God is in heaven. God is just. No one questioned that divine attribute. Job is righteous. Others do not know that though. Job's misfortune is understood as divine punishment for wrong-doing. Job wants a trial, convinced that if he can be judged in a tribunal of justice, tried before God, he will be vindicated. Job is certain that if he and God could meet as fellow human beings, the matter would be settled satisfactorily.

Suddenly an idea strikes Job like a bolt of lightning. For one brief, fleeting moment, the sufferer entertains a possibility that boggles the mind. If there could be an umpire, an arbiter, a mediator! If someone could stand between him and God. If someone positioned between Job and God could represent Job's alienation and God's holiness. That would do it. The problem would be solved.

Job's idea became Job's prayer. Job prays for a bridge that will link him to God. The prayer passes from Job's lips quickly, and it has Advent written all over it. Job's Advent prayer is a plea for God to provide an umpire, an arbiter, who can settle this dispute about his righteousness and facilitate a better relationship between him and God.

Apparently, from the looks of the biblical text, Job dismissed the thought of an umpire almost as quickly as he conceived it. Job breathes his prayer, then forgets it. No sooner does he speak his plea to God then he continues with his litany of complaints.

"What is the point?" you may be asking. Perhaps you are wondering if I have forgotten that this chapter on Job is a part of a book on Advent, a volume to encourage a meaningful journey to Christmas. How can help for that pilgrimage be derived from studying a man slumped atop a garbage heap, covered with sores, and troubled in his soul? More pointedly, how can any unanswered prayer be considered a blessing? How can God's failure to grant the request of an Advent prayer be interpreted as a benefit of the season?

Feeling wrongly accused, Job asked for a trial in a court of law. He sought to appease God's anger. He wanted someone to stand between God in heaven and his place in a ditch. Job demanded arbitration, an umpire, and would gladly have settled for a small indication of God's justice. God answered Job out of a whirlwind. Though Job didn't get exactly what he expected from God, he got what he needed—a new perspective.

Job's dilemma is really the dilemma of humanity. We want justice, vindication, and mediation. As with Job, God didn't answer as we expected. God did even more. Instead of giving us what we want, God sent us what we need—a Savior.

God answers with acceptance based on grace. Jesus comes and reveals God's love. God sends not just a mediator to settle a complaint but a Redeemer to implement the divine plan. God sets arbitration aside and offers salvation. God reveals in Jesus an infinite compassion for all of creation and boundless mercy.

The blessing of Advent is a reminder that God forever gives more than we can know about, much less request. Who could have envisioned and prayed for Christmas as God conceived it and gave it? We might have expected Christ's birth to be revealed to a few devout people busy with their prayers. They could have written about it or offered a press release. Eventually, everybody would have heard and felt good about it. But no! Angels announced the birth of Jesus to shepherds who stopped what they were doing and set out to find the child. A small sign would have been nice. People might find joy in searching for such a sign. Again, no! God gave a star. God set a sign in the heavens. All who seek the Christ can find Him. A glimpse would satisfy most folks, just a peak at the Messiah.

Everybody understands that someone like Jesus (though there is no one else like Jesus) cannot be available to just anybody who needs Him. Maybe some people prayed for just a fleeting view. Thank God that prayer was not answered! God saw to it that people were offered not merely a *glimpse* of Christ but an opportunity for an ongoing, eternal relationship with Him.

I hope a major truth of Advent is becoming clearer. Sometimes an unanswered prayer is a blessing from God. All too often we ask God for less than we need and for less than God desires to give. Not even the greatest of messianic hopes came close to envisioning the nature of God's gift in Christ. None of our best hopes for the future can comprehend what God has in store for us.

During a journey through Advent, people's faith should open like a rosebud unfolding in the warmth of the sun. Appropriate to Advent is a desire on our part to receive what God wants to give, not just a wish to get what we ask for. Advent is a time for praying expansively, rejecting narrow visions, and doing away with confining expectations. On our journey to Christmas we will do well not to deprive ourselves of all that God has to offer.

We pray for a joyful season. God wants to provide an abundant life. We pray for the release of political prisoners. God desires the liberation of all people suffering bondage of any kind. We pray for a means of escape from a dreaded problem. God offers a way for us to deal with all problems. We pray that we will not get caught in an act of wrongdoing. God grants forgiveness for wrongdoing and an incentive to doing right. We pray for peace between nations. God makes available peace for all people. We pray for a full recognition of the Christ who came to Bethlehem. God makes possible a redemptive confrontation with the Christ who comes to our world.

No, the traditional pageantry of Advent is not in Job. But present here are the kind of people who long for Advent—the God of Advent. Anyone of us could be named "Job." We can identify with his plight and passion. We have prayed surrounded by all kinds of garbage, frustrated by our friends, distraught by problems, and pained by sores. The God who hears Job hears us. Like Job, we receive from God more than we request. We discover among God's gifts a quality of help that we could not have anticipated.

Maybe reading about Job will cause us to open up. Perhaps we can travel the rest of the way to Christmas more receptive to whatever God is doing and to all that God has to offer. Perhaps, from now on, our prayers will not be about just one thing but about everything—that is, everything that really matters. We may discover that some of our prayers from the past have gone unanswered in order that the bigger prayers inspired by Advent can be answered. What a blessing!

O come, O come, Emmanuel.

A Prayer of Commitment

Luke 1:38, 46-55

The Faith of Advent

*H*ow does Christmas come? Clocks, calendars, and almanacs do not tell the whole story. A day or a season can come and go apart from any meaningful celebration. Ask any spouse who has forgotten a wedding anniversary.

How does Christmas come? Force will not assure its arrival. Nor will desire. For some people, Christmas is like an impossible dream. They always desire it but never feel they really experience it. Others have not given up on force. They want to enjoy a happy Christmas so much that they attempt to make it happen. These folks close their eyes to bills, diagnoses, and due dates in order to think only of candles and ribbons. They close their ears to typewriters, phones, and requests for help so as not to be distracted from the tunes of carols.

Such individuals carefully measure their words to sound happy and fix their faces to look happy. None of it works. Over and over I hear people confess, "I just can't seem to get into the Christmas spirit. I listen to Christmas music and put up Christmas decorations, but I don't seem to be a part of any of it." Christmas does not come by desire or force.

How then? How does Christmas come? Christmas cannot be bought. Of course, most anyone with modest financial resources can purchase the trappings of Christmas. A family can make everything around them look like Christmas even if they do not experience it. Other folks, including friends, can be fooled. A Christmas tree, decorations, and impressively wrapped packages suggest that a family is really into Christmas. Members of

123

the family, though, know the truth and feel the terrible void that seems to be made uglier by the glitter surrounding them. Christmas is not for sale.

How does Christmas come? The correct answer to that question appears in the Advent prayer to which the attention of this chapter is devoted. In fact, so profoundly does this prayer answer that question that the one who prayed it, a person not even looking for Christmas, was completely overcome by the event. The prayer was first offered to God as a song.

Mary could have missed Christmas. Other New Testament personalities missed it. This young lady was confronted by the possibility of Christmas in a surprising manner. An angel said to Mary, "You will conceive in your womb and bear a son, and you shall call his name Jesus" (Luke 1:31). Understandably, Mary was troubled and afraid. She blurted out obvious questions: "How can Christmas come to this world? More specifically, how can Christmas ever come for a person like me?" Those were not her exact words. According to the New Testament, Mary actually said, "How can this be since I have no husband?" (v. 34) The meaning is the same. Christmas looked like an impossibility.

It still does. Given the chaos of our world and the conditions in our lives, Christmas looks like an impossibility. Our objections are loud and clear: We have no money. We have no peace. We have no hope. We have no friends. We have no gifts. How can Christmas come? We are asking what Mary was asking.

From the angel who appeared to Mary comes the message that God will see to it that Christmas comes. Mary was told, "The Holy Spirit will come upon you" (v. 35). For Mary, this meant that she would bear a son though still a virgin. For the Israelites, this meant that persons in bondage would be set free. For us, this means that sins can be forgiven, anxieties can be resolved, hope can be born, peace can arrive, and Christmas can come. None of this was or is humanly possible. Do not overlook the comment of the angel, though, "with God nothing will be impossible" (v. 37). Christmas is an act of God!

All of Mary's objections were lost in divine assurances. Mary did not understand all that God was doing but she was ready to be a part of it. Her statement is an amazing model of confidence and commitment in relation to God, "I am the handmaid of the Lord; let it be to me according to your word" (v. 38).

A handmaid was a female servant. Mary was offering herself for service. With no details, with no signed contract, Mary declared, "Whatever God says, I accept. Whatever God wants me to do, I'm ready."

How would she explain her pregnancy? What would she do with the child? How could she provide? Mary asked none of the predictable questions. The latter part of the first chapter of Luke and most of the second chapter cannot be understood apart from Mary's remark in 1:38. Mary simply said to God, "Let it be to me according to your word!"

Christmas came for Mary because of commitment. Faith! Sure, it was God's doing, but it required Mary's cooperation. God needed Mary. And God could use Mary only if she had an active faith.

Is this to imply that Jesus would not have been born had Mary not made a positive response to God? No. God finds a way for divine work to be done. If not in an inn, then in a stable. If the Christ is not safe in Bethlehem, then in Egypt. Ultimately, God would not have been stopped in sending Jesus into the world, but God did need Mary and her availability would have been inadequate without her obedience.

Mary's commitment made Christmas possible. An act of human faith paved the way for a redemptive act of God. A servant on earth became a servant of God and birthed the long-awaited Suffering Servant who would bring God and God's people together.

Christmas comes with commitment. Persons who view Christmas with cool objectivity and seek to observe it passively may miss it. Christmas cannot be understood, appreciated, or enjoyed from the outside. Only through total, personal involvement in Christmas can it be truly experienced. That involvement stems from faith, arises out of commitment. Christmas comes to people who are willing to be God's servants. People like Mary.

We cannot force Christmas. We cannot buy Christmas. We can only *faith* it!

Superficial celebrations are needless and worthless. No one has to fake Christmas. To experience the spirit of the season, people do not have to blot out daily problems, family difficulties, and individual struggles. Difficult situations do not deter Christ. Christ appears in the middle of tough times; He shows up where there is no light and takes up residence where there is no music. He is the source of the Christmas spirit. What Christ offers cannot be experienced by whipping ourselves into an escapist trance in which we see nothing but candles and hear nothing but silver bells. Christmas comes only with Christ. Christmas is recognized and received by means of commitment.

We cannot force Christmas to come. We cannot wish Christmas into existence. We cannot purchase Christmas. But we can *faith* it. Christmas is no fragile dream to be protected from interruptions that threaten to destroy it. Christmas is a basic reality to be grasped only by faith.

Receiving Christmas as a gift is difficult for many people. By nature and training, we are doers, movers, and pushers. We are accustomed to making things happen when we want them to happen. We set our minds to achieve certain goals, work hard, and accomplish our aims. So if we want Christmas, we will work hard. We will make ourselves sing carols until we feel better. We will throw parties and insist that everybody have a good time. Christmas defies such manipulative pressure.

Christmas comes only as a gift to be received by faith. Christmas does not arrive as a result of frantic activities. The great New Testament scholar C. H. Dodd once described faith as "an act which is the negation of all activity, a moment of passivity out of which the strength for action comes, because in it God acts." His words not only get at the essence of faith but also point to the manner in which Christmas is experienced.

Open, vulnerable receptivity is difficult for action-oriented, impatient, I'll-get-what-I-want people, but that is the posture essential to an experience of Christmas. Christmas is a gift from God to be received by way of a commitment to live as God's servant. To live by faith.

Yet a warning is in order. The faith which brings Christmas involves much more than Christmas. Getting into this joyous season can get people into more than they have bargained for. True commitment is unconditional. Exercising faith can thrust the faithful into extremely difficult situations. Look at Mary.

In the words of Mary's prayer-song, usually called the Magnificat, the nature of her faith is revealed. It is a Christmas faith and more. For Mary, a commitment to fulfilling God's purpose is not a myopic, romantic feeling fed by singing angels and worshiping shepherds. It is a tough-willed acceptance of God's intent to reorder all of life.

> He [God] has scattered the proud in the imagination
>   of their hearts,
> he has put down the mighty from their thrones,
> and exalted those of low degree;
> he has filled the hungry with good things,
> and the rich he has sent empty away (Luke 1:51-53).

Radical! In Mary's mind, doing God's will involves loving lonely people, giving respect to despised persons, and feeding those who are hungry. A trip around the neighborhood to sing carols or a few visits with strangers to share Christmas baskets is not enough. A person's total life-style must be involved. Proceeding with care is wise. A happy acceptance of Christ in the manger could end up demanding that we share in Christ's cross.

How does Christmas come? Mary answers that question. For her Christmas came because of God's action and her cooperation with God's action in faith. Both were needed—what God did and what she did. Her commitment made Christmas possible. It will be no different for us.

God wants to use us. Christ wants to take form in us. Mary's situation precisely. For us, Christmas comes not in standing back to admire what happened in the past but in opening ourselves to what God wants to be doing in us in the present. Christmas comes for us through our involvement in God's action—making ourselves available as servants and offering our lives as mangers. Faith is required. Commitment is essential.

For some people, Christmas will come only if the Savior's birth is celebrated by their personal acceptance of the Savior as their Lord. Joy, real Christmas joy, will explode as their sins are forgiven in an encounter with Christ. God will do the seemingly impossible again—change a life that had become set in its ways, remove guilt that seemed unshakable, precipitate love amid hatred, and instill the peace of Christ where chaos had ruled.

For others, Christmas will come only if God is again acknowledged as sovereign and obeyed accordingly. God is ready to act in people's lives today just as in Mary's life yesterday. God is willing to use us in special ways. However, God respects our freedom and refuses to treat us as puppets. God awaits our acceptance of the divine will, our invitation to receive divine leadership.

How does Christmas come? Read the Magnificat again. In the text of that Advent prayer-song, Mary points the way to Christmas, the way Christmas comes to us. Commitment is the key. The best reception of Christ and response to Christ is a confession of His Lordship that results in faithful discipleship, personal faith, and an individual encounter with Christ. Joseph Fletcher's words make the point poignantly:

> Even if Christ were to be born a thousand times in a thousand stables laid in a thousand mangers and in a thousand Bethlehems, unless he is born in our own hearts through our own responsive love, our gratitude responding to his redemptive love, we do not have the faith of the incarnation.[19]

And we do not know Christmas. Christmas does not come.

Mary's Advent prayer is of extreme importance. God answers such a prayer. Nothing less than all of life is at stake.

To offer a prayer consistent with the nature of the Advent season is to request that God act in us and through us. We must commit ourselves unreservedly to participate in what God is doing in this world. Praying during Advent means inviting God into our lives as well as into our world and promising to live with God right here.

Mary's prayer changed her life and brought Christ—and thus Christmas—to her world. This prayer appropriated and sincerely offered by us, will do no less in our lives.

"Let it be to me according to your word."

O come, O come, Emmanuel.

Prayers of Praise

Luke 2:13-14, 28-32

The Joy of Advent

A lmost every year the same thing happens. Advent has been meaningful, fulfilling, and inspirational. Personal spirituality has been nurtured profoundly by the sights and sounds of celebration. Reminders of God's faithfulness in keeping promises have been received as good gifts. Reflections on God's revelations in the past have strengthened hope and heightened an anticipation of a God-dominated future. Then comes the last week of Advent, the days immediately prior to Christmas Day.

By all logic the fourth week of Advent should be characterized by the highest expressions of Christmas worship—majestic choral music, resounding confessions of faith, a sermon which stirs the soul, commitments to Christian discipleship, extravagant offerings to God in the name of the child adored by kings. Just prior to Christmas Day we should be ready to unleash our emotions, to pull out all the stops on the organ, and to celebrate the birth of the Christ child with unrestrained enthusiasm, unparalleled beauty, and a proliferation of praise. Almost everyone is ready for the familiar texts of the second chapter of Luke. But the way it should be is not always the way it is.

Honestly, for me, preparation for Christmas during the fourth week of Advent is often the most difficult work of the entire season. Writing this chapter has been no exception. Unlike previous weeks, words do not come to mind quickly. I have a sense of coming to the very brink of joy, creeping to the edge of the Christmas festival, then stumbling, stopping in my tracks, and not knowing how to do justice to the announcement of the ages.

The problem is not unique to me. Living is the issue, and that is everybody's concern. What do you do as you approach the city limits of Bethlehem just prior to Christmas? How does anybody know what is best to do or best to say at this point? How can we discuss Christmas so that everyone will know the subject is not merely a repetitive seasonal interruption of routines but the most basic reality of life? Complicating our dilemma is the truth that most of us know a great deal more about an anticipation of deliverance and a hope of divine disclosure than we do about an actual, direct divine revelation in our midst.

The prayers of previous weeks may have come rather easily. Who could not identify with a troubled prophet at his wit's end screaming to God, "Why don't you tear the sky open and come down?" (Isa. 64:1, GNB). I have been there. I know that feeling of frustration and desperation. So do most people. Then there was Job who seems like an older brother. Just like that tormented man from Uz, we have felt so burdened by the apparent silence of God that we have scaled down our requests to God—praying for less than we need, asking for less than God wants us to have. We have willingly compromised our praying because of a nagging desire to hear anything from God—anything at all to indicate that God is still there. The reminders contained in Mary's prayer song are always beneficial. We cannot force an act of God even in regard to Christmas but only receive it as a gift and respond to it in faith. Those prayers have been easy enough to understand and to embrace. They were never problematic even if sometimes they were painful. The words in those prayers come from where we live.

What is next is different. My own experience is with heavens unopened, with stars which do not move and with promises which, for the most part, go unfulfilled. I have much less trouble identifying with a man shouting at the darkened night skies in frustration than imagining folks looking to skies filled with angels singing in jubilation. I am far more familiar with the garbage dumps of life than with stables in which worshipers bow before a manger, singing. That is the problem. I can write about the pathos of life. I know it well, too well. But that is not the subject at this point in the Advent pilgrimage.

When the need is greatest and the time most appropriate to capture the essence of Christmas in words, I find that the Word which became flesh defies human words. Maybe that is as it should be. Perhaps our preparation as we approach the pinnacle of this season should not be easy.

Thank goodness for the second chapter of Luke. Here are the words to shore up our stumbling thoughts and mumbled comments. Luke helps us to say what we do not know how to say and to declare what we cannot declare on our own. Once again, prayer texts are of prime importance.

Luke's infancy narrative contains several different prayers, but two invite special consideration at this point. Ponder carefully the prayer of the heavenly hosts and the prayer of the elderly Simeon.

The prayer of the angels is of cosmic proportions. Just reading it generates a sense that the entire universe is involved in voicing these words. Rightly so, creation and redemption are both involved in this moment. Angels sing in response to God's ultimate revelation. The heavenly hosts herald the possibility of a new creation.

Simeon's prayer is much more particular, more personal. This elderly man who has tightly gripped one strong hope for a lifetime finally sees the realization of his most cherished dreams. He cannot contain his emotions.

Joy fills the heavens and floods the earth. Unconditional happiness among heavenly beings is met by happiness among inhabitants of the world. Antiphonal "Hallelujahs" ring out. Music resounds in people's hearts and rolls across their lips. The Messiah is born! Adoration abounds. "Glory to God in the highest!" (Luke 2:14).

Now, a pause. The matter of Advent joy needs more attention. Frequently, people speak of the elusive nature of the joy of this season. Already I have confessed my own inability to grasp it firmly or to define it satisfactorily. In the prayer of the angels is an insight which can be very instructive. Maybe we have had difficulty with joy because we have looked for it in the wrong places.

Ask people what it would take for them to know joy and likely you will get a quick response. Most people have long lists of what they need to experience joy. One prerequisite for joy is right there in the angels' prayer—peace on earth. What rejoicing there would be if international peace could be assured. Free the political hostages, dismantle the weapons, sign the treaties, and discharge the armies. Joy will erupt.

The very idea of peace between nations sets off thoughts about peace between persons, peace within families, and peace among co-workers. Then speculation turns to internal peace—the possibility of illnesses cured, anxieties calmed, security realized, and faith discovered so that a person can know peace within. That kind of peace would inspire singing for sure.

Read again the prayer which the angels sang. "Glory to God in the highest." Notice that was the first declaration of the heavenly host, not the second. Now set this statement in its historical context. A less than loving king ruled that region of the world. People were heavily, many would say unjustly, taxed. One self-acclaimed messiah after another had appeared, attracted followers, failed at a revolution, and been killed. People knew no peace.

The shepherds to whom the angels appeared were in an even worse situation than most other people. Nobody respected shepherds. They were social and religious outcasts. But look. The angels appeared to shepherds and their chorus of "Glory to God in the highest" rang out across that desolate land on the back side of nowhere.

Did you catch the insight about joy? Joy was found through participation in the divine event, not in external circumstances. In the prayer of the angels, words about peace followed, not preceded, words of joy. Words about peace were not prerequisites for joy. Peace came from joy. That is the divine order of things. Such also is the nature of Christmas liturgy. Praise to God comes first.

The old divines were correct in their declaration that the chief end of every person is to glorify God. Praise to God creates the posture and establishes the spirit in which salvation can be received and lives altered. No higher priority exists than ascribing praise to God.

But praising God does not mean ignoring the world. Just the

opposite. Divine revelation *always* has both a vertical and a horizontal dimension. Look again at the prayer of the angels.

Peace on earth and peace in human hearts, contributors to great joy among people, come from a proper adoration of God. That is not the end of the matter, however. A truly joyful person is an aggressive peacemaker. People who praise God sincerely seek to help each other compassionately.

The angels' prayer presents a pattern to be reflected in life. Praise to God comes first, but peacemaking and loving (peace and persons of goodwill) inevitably follow. Joy is to be found amid the adoration of God and a ministry of reconciliation among people.

Simeon saw the truth of the angels' prayer. Ironically, now that he knew the Christ had come, Simeon felt he could die in peace. Why? Wouldn't knowing Christ had been born create in Simeon a desire for life to continue? Simeon had seen the glory of God in the face of the baby Jesus. He no longer had any doubts that life on earth would begin to change—for the better. The praise of God invariably sets in motion efforts which enhance the nature of the human situation.

Advent joy, the joy of which the angels sang at Jesus' birth, joy as a result of the proper praise of God, relates to external conditions but does not depend upon them. Joy persists whether contemplating life or facing death. Because of the internal joy, a possibility always exists that in cooperation with God external conditions can be altered.

The text of the angels' prayer in Luke's Gospel conveys the meaning of Christmas and frees us of difficulties produced if we misunderstand our task during the days just before Christmas Day. Ponder the prayer. Make it your own, if you will. We need feel no special pressure to say just the right words and to take just the right actions because Christmas Day is close at hand. We do not have to *create* the joy of this day either for ourselves or others. What a relief! The joy is a given.

The presence of problems does not silence expressions of joy. Christmas is coming. Christ first came to a troubled world, and He still does. Advent joy does not exist despite problems but as a source of strength for dealing with problems. We do not need to feel any responsibility in relation to ourselves or to others to blot out all thoughts of problems in order to guarantee a proper celebration of Christmas. We couldn't do that if we had to. Ours is the happy privilege of accepting joy and announcing joy ("good news of great joy") even in the midst of trouble. It is not a matter of positive thinking or playing a seasonal mind game. Christ presents that joy.

A joyful celebration of Christmas is possible. Not because of what we have done to get ready for it. Not because this year we finally got our act together. Not because our shopping has been finished early, worship services attended regularly, and relationships nurtured happily. The joy of Christmas is not our doing. The reason for joy in this season resides in the redemptive action of God.

We are called to join God's action of redemption. God calls us to accept what only God can provide. God offers salvation. God invites all of creation to an experience of faith. Little wonder that gratitude is the response. "Great God!" "Holy God!" "Good God!" Or, to quote the angels, "Glory to God in the highest."

Our reservations about the arrival of Christmas Day recede as our protests about preparedness are muted. Who dares say, "Wait, Lord. The time is not yet right. Many in our community are sick and still more are troubled. We sense no peace in our hearts and we are dead sure about the absence of peace on this planet. Wait, Lord. We can feel better about Christmas if you will let us have a little longer to strengthen our families, to improve our citizenship in the community, to initiate a greater faithfulness to our church, and to do some work on reconciliation"? (My guess is that a lot of people think as much even if the words are never spoken.) The divine clock is striking. God is inviting people to salvation. Already angels are singing.

God's revelation is before us and His invitation to us has "RSVP" written all over them. We have to respond—now. Christmas is upon us. We cannot wait.

Most likely what we do at Christmas will not be very different from what we do at other times. We can choose to keep on tightly clutching life, striving to work out everything for the better by our own efforts, planning one day to stand before God and to offer joy as a gift that will cause divine pride. Or we can decide to let go of our death grip on life, acknowledge our inability to work out much of anything on our own, bow down before God in adoration, and receive joy as God's gift to us.

Listen! God's clock is striking. Look! God's presence is among us. Respond! Receive the Christ. Free excited emotions to express unrestricted praise. Do not hinder convicted souls from making life-changing commitments. This is no time for restraint. Openly accept the joy which comes from heaven and faithfully share this joy throughout the earth. Glory to God in the highest and on earth peace among people of goodwill.

Christ has been born. Christ is being born. Christ waits to be born.

O come, O come, Emmanuel!

PART V

CHRISTMAS: CELEBRATING THE BIRTH OF THE SAVIOR

"Glory to God in the highest" (Luke 2:14).

Jesus Has Come!
And He Shall Reign!
Forever and Ever!

CHAPTER 16

Jesus Has Come!

*I*mmediately after George F. Handel had written the last lines of the "Hallelujah Chorus," someone clumsily ventured into his room. The magnificent musical work lay finished before the composer. With tears streaming down his face, Handel exclaimed, "I did think I did see all heaven before me, and the great God himself."[20]

Handel provides the vision for today and the emotion for this moment. Christmas is here. Jesus has come!

Matthew makes the announcement rather matter-of-factly, "Jesus was born in Bethlehem of Judea in the days of Herod the king" (2:1). Luke states the truth pastorally, "And she gave birth to her first-born son. . . . to you is born this day in the city of David a Savior, who is Christ the Lord" (2:7, 11). John presents the good news somewhat philosophically, "And the Word became flesh and dwelt among us" (1:14). Paul writes of the Savior's birth theologically, "But when the time had fully come, God sent forth his Son" (Gal. 4:4). All of it means the same and points to one truth. Jesus has come.

Jesus Christ has been born. The Messiah has arrived. Little wonder that Handel thought he caught a glimpse of God. How right the composer was to respond with a chorus of hallelujahs. What else could be said? Anyone who fully realizes the truth of the incarnation—God is with us, Jesus has come—will respond with a hallelujah or some similar expression.

But what does this truth mean? What is the significance of affirming Christ's birth? Christmas is a time for joyful singing and enthusiastic celebrations—

during these weeks hallelujahs come easily. But Christmas is more than a season for feeling good. Enthusiasm during Christmas is not an end in itself. What is the meaning of the truth that provokes the joy, the excitement, the hallelujahs?

Amid the raucous enthusiasm of Christmas, pause for a moment and ponder the truth that has set all of this in motion. If you can, briefly discard all of the decorations and symbols of the season that surround you in order to focus without distraction on the stark reality of the incarnation. I do not wish to mute a single Christmas hallelujah, but I do wish to encourage a full recognition of why hallelujahs are appropriate.

He has come. Jesus has come! How can we take it in? The truth is almost too much for us. Before another hallelujah is spoken, roll over in your mind, seek to embrace with your intellect, subject to the intricacies of your imagination, and sense with your emotions the meaning of that statement—Jesus has come. Think what it means.

We Are Loved

By far the best biblical text for Christmas is John 3:16. John records the meaning of God's act of incarnation for the human situation. God loved. "God so loved the world." We are the world. We are the recipients of God's love. To declare about Christ, "He has come" is to confess about ourselves, "We are loved."

The revelation of God's love for all people is a person. No long-distance telephone call from God or divinely dictated telegram would do. Pretty leaflets imprinted with a sentimental poem on the Deity's love could have been dropped from the heavens and scattered by the wind, but, no, the message of God's compassion was conveyed through God's Son.

We know God's love not through a bombastic, intimidating miracle that sends shock waves throughout the universe, but by way of a cooing, inviting baby born in a stable in Bethlehem. God loved us enough to appear among us. God loves us enough to live with us. The apostle Paul was staggered by this truth, and his awe is apparent as he writes of Christ: "Who, though he was in the form of God, [he] did not count equality with God a thing to be grasped, but emptied himself, taking the form of a servant, being born in the likeness of men" (Phil. 2:6-7).

Bethlehem holds significance for us. This tiny village was the site of Jesus' birth physically and historically. At the same time Bethlehem is a symbol of Jesus' presence among us personally and spiritually. Jesus comes into our little worlds. Christ can take form in the out-of-the-way places in our lives. No part of our existence is beyond God's love.

Jesus acts among us in our world today just as He did in the first century. He accepts children whom others push aside. He takes into His heart those hurts that prevent happiness. He sensitively touches lepers, victims of AIDS, and others from whom most people retreat. He heals sicknesses in people's souls, elevates the downtrodden, reconciles ruptured relationships, and restores wholeness to fragmented personalities. He loves us.

We are loved! We are loved by God. God loves even the unlovable. More accurately stated, God finds in everybody that which is lovable. God comes to us. God comes to be with us, to hear us out, to touch us, and to take us in. Jesus is God's definition of love.

Jesus has come! That means we are loved. Loved by God. Hallelujah! Jesus' birth also means . . .

Time Is Filled with Opportunity

The birth of Jesus took place in one moment of time—a specific year, month, day, hour, and minute. No one knows the exact moment, but that one moment in time made *all* time important. Something significant happened. Jesus' birth in Bethlehem of Judea filled all time with meaning. To this day, time is filled with opportunity because of what happened in that one superlative moment of divine ministry.

Dionysius Exiguus devised our system of using B.C. and A.D. with years. Exiguus divided history at the point of Christ's birth, thus underscoring that event as *the* watershed in human history. With the birth of Jesus, promise became fulfillment. The significance of time changed when the whisper, "Jesus is coming," gave way to the shout, "Jesus has come!"

With the birth of the Savior, eternity broke into history. God's time invaded our time. Heaven touched earth. Eternal life is no longer a faint hope. The arrival of Jesus endowed every subsequent moment with the potential to serve as a bridge to eternity. Truly celebrating Christmas Day is akin to standing on top of a mountain from which we can see a broader view of life and breathe purer air.

When he was a young boy, on one occasion Archbishop William Temple deplored the fact that he had so much to do and so little time in which to do it. In response, his father offered a bit of wise counsel that is applicable to everybody. "William," he said, "You have all the time there is."[21] Right. We all do. Time is available to experience the birth of Jesus. Within time, present time, a person can lay hold of a quality of life that is best called "eternal."

Jesus has come! Think of it. Time, all of time, is filled with opportunity, but even that piece of good news does not tell the whole story. The fact that Jesus has come means that...

Light Does Break

When Advent began, we knew we needed the season. Unspeakable tragedies had traumatized us. Sharp disappointments had distressed us. Unanswered questions of profound importance troubled us. Harmful habits enslaved us. Relentless demands demoralized us. We needed help. We asked for guidance. We longed for light. Most often, though, light seemed so scarce that we decided our eyes must make a permanent adjustment to darkness.

We read of people in the past who, while walking in darkness, saw a great light. Honestly, though, we feel no identity with those early pilgrims. Our journey is shrouded in darkness and bombarded with questions. When will answers appear? When will peace be established? When will hope find even minimal fulfillment? When, if ever, will light break? We cry with Habakkuk, a prophet with a kindred spirit, "O Lord, how long?" (1:2).

God responds. Jesus' birth is the assurance that light does break—if not immediately, at least eventually. Light will come because Christ has come. Of course, light may not shine at the precise point of our demand. The sun does not rise according to our schedules, but the sun does rise. Light breaks.

Accompanying that assurance is a warning. No lesser light can suffice for Christ's light. Substitutes do not help. We cannot reproduce the sun. Or the Son. Unfortunately, people who need a brilliant beacon settle for a flickering candle. The light of Christmas can be known only in the Christ, but that light can be known.

Because of this truth, Martin Luther once said that he felt he could run out of the dark house of his life into the sunshine. True. Everybody can. However, for multitudes of people the possibility of light does not seem so immediate or dramatic. John Bunyan's main character in *The Pilgrim's Progress* speaks for us. Seeking directions for his journey, Christian asks Evangelist for guidance. Evangelist responds with a question, "Do you see yonder shining light?" Note carefully Christian's answer. "I think I do!" [22] We understand.

Christmas is here. Festivities abound. Yet we're not all that sure about the defeat of darkness. We want to believe. We *think* we see light.

In Bunyan's masterpiece, Evangelist says, "Keep that light in your eye, and go up directly thereto."[23] So, like our brother pilgrim, we focus on that light and walk toward it. Today we can see it clearly enough to follow it. As we celebrate Christmas and the light that has come, we pray that fear will depart and along our journey the light will become brighter and brighter.

Jesus has come. The meaning is unmistakable. Light breaks on, in, and around us. Hallelujah.

We Can Be Redeemed

God never gives up on life. Creation has provided the Creator plenty of reasons to give up on it. People have disdained God and veritably invited destruction. However, not once has God wavered in the divine resolve to offer redemption. Nowhere is that divine resolution clearer than in the incarnation. Because Jesus has come, all people are given the privilege of repentance, the offer of forgiveness, and the grace of redemption. To paraphrase a promise from Jesus, because He lives, we can live.

The infant of Christmas Day became the man of Passion Week. A child secretly escorted into Egypt to prevent His death became a man who rode boldly into Jerusalem to accept His death. Skies once brightened by angels heralding Christ's birth were blackened by storm clouds as all of creation mourned Christ's crucifixion. The best God could offer was crucified by the worst humankind could offer. The manger and the cross both point to the divine intention that all people be confronted by the opportunity for loving redemption.

We can be redeemed! That is the great good news of Christmas. In Christ's teaching we find the way for living. In Christ's dying we discover the way for loving. In Christ's compassion we encounter the source of our redemption.

Jesus has come! We can be redeemed. Hallelujah!

CHAPTER 17

And He Shall Reign!

*D*irectly across the street from Manger Square in Bethlehem stands the Church of the Nativity. The front entrance to that place of worship is only about four feet high. In the past, large animals like cattle, horses, and camels created a problem by wandering into the building. The low entrance was constructed to prevent such unwelcome intruders. Today, most people have to bend very low to enter the traditional site of Jesus' birth. How appropriate! That is the posture for Christmas. Approaching the event of incarnation, we should be bent in reverent adoration.

As Advent began, we were well aware of our need for the season. As the four weeks of Advent passed, we read the Bible, prayed, sang, hoped, worshiped, made commitments, and in other ways sought to get ready for Christmas. The promise of Jesus' coming—then and now—kept us going. Christmas came with its mind-boggling announcement "Jesus has come!" Celebrations erupted. Life was fun. Faith was strong. Then what? Is it all over? No! In no sense is it over. It never will be all over.

At Christmas divinely inspired words of Scripture must also be heard. "He shall reign!" Jesus shall reign. The One who came to Bethlehem by way of Mary's womb, taking on life as a baby, eventually emerges from a post-crucifixion-resurrection tomb as the eternal Savior and the everlasting Lord of all life, and He shall reign!

He shall reign! No sooner are the words spoken than they precipitate questions. He shall reign? Really? Why then the persistence of war? What about senseless deaths? Does His kingdom have a place for cancer cells? What about the continual triumph of evil over good? Jesus reigns? Come on. Get serious.

Truly celebrating Christmas means developing a new perspective on all of life. Troubles do not cease. Christmas does not provide an answer for all of life's tough questions. However, Christmas does nurture a perspective on life that is crucial. The birth of the Savior encourages us to look at all of life from the point of view which develops at the manger of the Christ child. That is difficult if not scandalous for most modern people. But the manger is the place to begin understanding life.

An analogy makes the point. Looking at a piece of fabric through a magnifying glass allows a person to catch sights that otherwise would be missed. A similar phenomenon accompanies views of life which start with the manger, Christmas.

The fabric at the center of a magnifying glass appears with great clarity. Details are readily apparent. However, at the periphery, the vision of the fabric is blurred and somewhat distorted. Similarly, when life is viewed through the central event of Christmas, a person can easily see what is important and what is true—even in great detail. The farther away from the manger people move, the more difficult it becomes to discern reality.

Look at life from the manger. View life from the perspective of Christ's birth and the eternal reign of Christ is clear. A study of the details of this truth establish the credibility of the vision. For example, readily apparent at Christmas is the fact that...

Humility Is Power

If you had a mandate to change the world for the better, how would you proceed? Carefully study political and military sciences. Seek counsel from experts in sociology. Open offices in Washington, D.C., Peking, Moscow, Nairobi, Johannesburg, Geneva, London, Buenos Aires, and Rio de Janeiro. Employ a staff of international consultants. Launch a campaign to win the confidences and votes of people around the world. Learn to manipulate the media. Be prepared to play "hard-ball politics" if necessary.

Look again.

God's strategy to change the world for the better began with the birth of a baby. The event, nonpolitical in nature, was a public relations nightmare. The birth took place in an inconspicuous place at an inconvenient time. God sought people's hearts rather than their votes. Leadership was defined in terms of servanthood. God, too, was concerned with power, but it was a different kind. God demonstrated once and for all that true power resides in humility.

You may be choking back a protest, about to explode with, "Power in humility! That is the stuff of dreams!" Think, though, before you reject God's strategy outright. What power have you ever known that rivals the power involved in the incarnation? What event other than the birth of Jesus has divided history, brought out singing angels, and made possible salvation for all people? Do you know a similar phenomenon? What act of humankind even comes close to this act of God? Remember, it all started at a manger.

In one of his many works, W. H. Auden has shepherds gather around the manger of Jesus and declare:

Tonight for the first time the prison gates
Have opened.
Music and sudden light
Have interrupted our routine tonight,
And swept the filth of habit from our hearts.
Oh here and now our endless journey starts.[24]

Is any other event so love-captivating, so obedience-commanding, and so life-altering?

True community, like authentic existence, arises around the manger. The numbers involved may be small. Real leadership and a strategy of love may attract only the shepherds of the neighborhood. Though thousands of people do not flock to the side of the baby servant, it is enough if only twelve are there, even if one is a potential traitor. God affirms humility as the true posture of power.

Anyone looking at life from a perspective far removed from Christmas, viewing existence through the periphery of a magnifying glass, will probably miss this truth. However, for those whose line of sight on life carries them through Bethlehem, the center of vision, it is perfectly clear. Hard to miss, in fact.

Start at the manger and you will see that Jesus has come. There, too, you will learn that He shall reign, and, as you watch the Christ child and ponder the meaning of His birth, you will discover that humility is power. That is not all. You will see as well the truth that...

Love Is Triumphant

Bowing before the infant Messiah nestled in the manger, we discover depths of love and breadths of its meaning that we have not previously imagined. God's love was behind this baby. God's love was fleshed out in this child.

But the manger could not hold Jesus any more than divine love could be restricted to a stable. As a matter of fact, God's love was ceaselessly moving, expanding in outreach. No person could hold it back. Nothing could stop it. Shortly after His birth, Jesus was out of the manger. Only briefly did He remain a stranger in Egypt. He refused to be confined to a carpenter's bench in Nazareth. Not even the miracle-seeking loyalists of the Galilean villages could persuade Jesus to stay in one place long. He declined an invitation to return to the side of His mother, though that decision would have replaced conflict with peace. Jesus would not allow people to ban Him from Jerusalem. Threats from His enemies did not slow Jesus down for one second. Jesus, the incarnation of God's love, would not be stopped. God's love could not be confined—not by a manger, not by a cross, and not by a tomb.

Once again, look at life through the lens of Christmas. Authentic love is triumphant. Love, especially suffering love, is sovereign. That assertion must not be confused with poetic idealism or a romantic theory. Isaiah spoke of the sovereignty of love though mired in the depths of a depressing captivity. In a mood of joyous festivity, Luke practically shouted an endorsement of the triumphant nature of love. Not even physical persecution could keep John from heralding the superiority of love.

No one should ever surmise that the primacy and victory of love are restricted to the pastoral narratives of Luke's report on the birth of Jesus. The triumph of love is as apparent amid the blood and gore of Christian martyrdom at the time of the Revelation as on that quiet evening in Bethlehem when Mary birthed a child and laid Him in a manger.

The story of one group of early Christian disciples has fed my soul for years. These believers were led into the coliseum in Rome to be killed because of their faith in Christ. In that arena of death, they spoke victoriously of love and life. Onlookers were stunned by the Christians' testimony of triumph. Preparing to die, the Christians joyfully confessed, "We have lived and we have loved, and we shall live and we shall love again. Hallelujah!"[25]

They knew it. These people knew the truth that love is triumphant. They were not about to betray their love for Christ because they were confident that Christ was not about to betray His love for them. The Roman coliseum seems like a long way from the manger in Bethlehem, but the reality of Christmas pervaded the people in both places. Love was triumphant. Jesus has come. And He shall reign! Hallelujah!

CHAPTER 18

Forever and Ever!

*A*dvent is over. Christmas Day has come and gone. For well over a month we have traversed a boundary between the visible and the invisible. We have observed the plight of life in this world—sometimes tragic —as we have pondered God's promises about a better world. Intimidated by the evil evidenced in human conditions around us and impressed by the strength of the sin within us, we have wept. Simultaneously, overwhelmed by the divine compassion for us and deeply moved by the divine visitation to us, we have rejoiced. We have worshiped God.

At moments during Advent, significant breakthroughs seemed to occur: the annoying sounds of sirens blared by ambulances rushing people to the emergency rooms of hospitals were replaced by the quiet, almost indiscernible sounds of shepherds making their way to a manger in some stable; headlines filled with bad news gave way to angels in a lighted sky heralding the kind of good news which brings joy to all people; politically motivated threats of world destruction gave way to divinely inspired visions of peace and salvation; cynicism was silenced by hopefulness sung to the tune of a Christmas carol. Breakthroughs seemed to occur, but only momentarily. Back and forth we fluctuated as we journeyed between disgust with things as they are and delight with things as they can be; between depression over the changeless routines and exhilaration because of the promise of being surprised by joy.

During Advent we walked and worshiped, indeed we

lived on the boundary. Our observance of Advent and celebration of Christmas allowed us to taste real fulfillment and to sample true happiness. For a split second here and there we were convinced that life could be different, radically different; that the activities of this season reflected the most basic realities of existence. We came close to such a conclusion. Almost!

Now Advent is over. Christmas has been celebrated. In this situation, at the beginning of a new year, a critical situation develops. Already some folks have decided we need to return to more predictable patterns. Their reasoning rings with familiarity: sure, an occasional hallelujah was OK during Advent, and particularly close to Christmas Day, but if we keep on being so emotional people will think we've lost our minds.

We even feel pressure to put away the decorations of the season. We hurry to take down decorations and put everything back in order. The subtle assumption is that we are done with all of it—this Christmas thing—for another year.

"Wait! Wait! Don't do it! Please do not allow that to happen!" Everything within me screams those words. At Christmas, in Christ, God showed us what all of life is about. Advent is a special season but it should not be separate from that which precedes it and that which follows it. Christmas Day is no delightful diversion primarily for children.

Prior to moving away from this season and before concluding this book, one more word requires attention. Please do not miss it. We need it. The New Testament resounds with it. The word is *forever*.

Typically, immediately after Christmas many people are faced with a nostalgia that borders on mild depression. "It's over! I have enjoyed the holidays so much. I like the way the world looks and people behave during this season. Now I must wait another whole year to experience such happiness again."

Scripture soundly refutes such a conclusion. The trumpets of Advent rightly can sound throughout the year. The true light of Christmas cannot be extinguished by the breeze formed by turning the pages on a calendar. Nothing is over. More accurately, everything has just begun.

On the day after Christmas God does not take back divine promises, cease instilling visions of peace and feelings of goodwill, or halt the inspiration for shouting, "Hallelujah!" As the apostle Paul declares, "For all the promises of God find their Yes in him [Christ]" (2 Cor. 1:20). As John demonstrates, a real hallelujah has an eternal ring to it. In other words, all of the Advent truth which we have considered and the Christmas joy we have celebrated is forever. All of this, the promises on the preceding pages, is forever and ever.

The totality of life every day is to be lived on the boundary, at the intersection where God and the world meet, at the point at which God's eternal presence breaks into our personal history. Once we have been to Christmas—really been to Christmas, bowed before the manger, welcomed Christ into our hearts—no part of life ever again will be the same. From Christmas forward, we live somewhat on edge, never knowing when a star might appear to lead us or angels show up to sing to us. Having realized that in some unsuspecting moment we may have to drop everything and hurry off on a Bethlehem journey, we resolve to live daily with spontaneity. And we commit ourselves to living generously as well—bringing to the One who came anything which He needs and everything which He requests.

Not even beginning a new year gets life back to normal. The very definition of "normal" has changed. Though at first we thought we had been "beside ourselves" because of the incredible promises and joy of Advent, now we know we finally have discovered our true selves, claiming the promises and experiencing a joy that will never end.

"Forever!" That is God's commentary on Christmas. "Thine is the kingdom and the power and the glory for ever!" (Matt. 6:13). "I will be with you always" (28:20, GNB). Forever. Seek to sense the significance of that word. Play out in your mind its meaning for our lives.

God Offers Encouragement to Human Discouragement

Should that truth strike you as merely a seasonal cliché, be done with the thought. Encouragement from God is an eternal phenomenon. How I like that ascription of praise found in Psalm 3:3, "Oh Lord, my glorious One, who lifts up my head" (NIV). The *King James Version* renders the passage, "Thou, O Lord, art, . . . the lifter up of mine head." What a wonderful observation about God. Christmas is God's way of saying, "Lift up your heads. Do not give up on life regardless of how tough it gets. I am joining you in the midst of your days. We will face the future together."

From any other person such words would have a hollow ring. "All right, join me if you will. We will be discouraged together." However, the words are from God. The promise is of divine origin. The certainty of fulfillment can be seen in the nativity of Christ.

The God whom we serve is Lord of failures and disappointments as well as successes and happiness. God knows full well the kind of discouragement to which divine encouragement is compassionately directed. Before Jesus could get comfortable in the manger in Bethlehem, He had to be taken into Egypt to escape the violence of an angry, egocentric king. Not everybody flocked to the side of Jesus in adoration. Even some members of His own family eventually turned against Him. Jesus' divinely shaped path to redemption was a road leading to crucifixion. Yet Jesus Christ is Lord. God is Sovereign. A dastardly act of execution was transformed by God into a graceful plan of redemption. The Jesus of the manger in Bethlehem, the Jesus of the journey into Egypt, the Jesus of the cross at Calvary, is also the Jesus of the empty tomb. He is the one who comes to us, joins us, and encourages us. God working in Christ can take even the major disasters of life and convert them into experiences which strengthen life.

The encouragement of Jesus is no easy counsel, no flippant optimism, no shallow psychological trickery. Often we still have to deal with much that is bad while He points us to all that is good. Jesus helps us to see the best of days, having experienced the worst of days. Jesus enables us to envision the heights of life from a vantage point amid the depths of life.

Christmas is always such a good time of the year because people feel encouraged to pursue the most important aspects of life. Realizing that God believes in people like us enough to send Jesus to be born among us and to give His life for us, we feel ready to talk of sharing, caring, peacemaking, gift-giving, and selfless love.

But why should this be only at Christmas? Divine encouragement for love, peace, and joy is not limited to a season but conveyed in a gospel for all of our days. God's ministry of encouragement extends far beyond Christmas. Forever. That is how long God's encouragement lasts. At every moment we will be supported in our pursuit of life's highest priorities, essential goods—forever and ever.

God Offers Strength to Human Weakness

Sometimes I get tired of trying to do what is best—always thinking clearly, acting responsibly, and speaking helpfully. Do you? Often I see people whose thoughts are irrational, whose actions are irresponsible, and whose speech is casual, and I realize that these people are well-liked, successful, and apparently happy. *What's the use?* I find myself asking. I know I am not alone in such musings. The question is born out of fatigue and a sense of futility. Such a state of being is as vulnerable to temptation and hurt as is an open sore to infection.

Few, if any, times during the year are any busier than Advent. We tend to overextend ourselves severely. One party after another. A reception here; a dinner there. An open house, a special church service. Terribly busy. Ridiculously overextended. Yet study what happens. People find strength to keep going. That which otherwise might be draining actually becomes enriching. "Getting there" may be a problem, but "being there" offers the promise of fellowship and strength.

Here is an important insight into God's provision of strength. Peacemaking over the long haul drains the emotions, tires the body, and attracts few associates. Yet within peacemaking, blessed strength is to be found. Hungering and thirsting after righteousness takes a heavy toll. Yet Jesus said, "Blessed are those who hunger and thirst for righteousness" (Matt. 5:6). Extending forgiveness to someone who has offended or hurt you requires every ounce of energy and willpower available. Yet, as forgiveness is granted, strength is renewed.

What sounds at first like double-talk eventually is found to be straight-talk. The words came to Paul by way of Christ. The same message comes from God to us. "My power is strongest when you are weak" (2 Cor. 12:9, GNB). At Christmas we know the validity of that truth as at no other time, but it is not a seasonal promise. We can count on God's offer of strength regardless of the severity of our weakness. Always! This, too, is forever and ever.

God Offers Salvation to Human Lostness

God comes near to us during Advent, takes up residence among us during Christmas, and stays with us forever. Ironically, we keep trying to wander away from God. Invariably, we get into trouble. Out on our own, we meet temptations which we cannot handle. We get surrounded by darkness that we cannot dispel. The more we sense a need for fellowship, the more intense is the feeling that we are alone.

Søren Kierkegaard made a great deal of the fact that Jesus was born at night. The great philosopher recognized an eternal truth in this historical fact. Midday came at midnight when Jesus was born. That is the way life goes with God. Salvation comes precisely at the point of our greatest need. If Jesus' birth at Bethlehem occurred at just the right time, so does Jesus' entry into our lives. It does not have to be Advent! The coming of Jesus in the past assures us of the availability of His presence in the present and future. The divine provision for salvation made possible through Jesus is forever.

Often persons decry an apparent absence of God and bemoan the lack of adequate knowledge about God. Take care here. The truth affirmed during Advent and perfectly revealed at Christmas is that people can get as close to God as they desire and know God as intimately as they are willing to risk. God is available in Christ—if not in a manger, then in an office suite; if not in the arms of a young mother riding on a donkey bound for Egypt, then in the fuselage of a giant airliner racing down a runway taking off to some city; if not on the sheep-grazed plains around Bethlehem, then on the heavily trafficked thoroughfare which we travel to get home. At all of the points of human lostness, God offers salvation—not just when heralded by angels in a heavenly riot of joy, but even when needed by strugglers so burdened that they cannot speak. The salvation announced at Christmas is forever and ever.

One of the finest prompters for Advent worship, public or private, is Handel's musical masterpiece, *Messiah*. I love hearing Handel's music, and I benefit greatly from reading his arrangement and treatment of the biblical text. During Advent I turn to Handel's work again and again. Little wonder, the whole salvation story is there.

Handel knew well the primacy of the word *forever* in relation to all of God's promises. The great composer singled out the word, set it to music, and triumphantly hurled it into the consciences of all who enjoy the benefits of his labor. Forever! Nowhere is the forever nature of the Christ-event more apparent and more splendidly stated than in Handel's soul-stirring "Hallelujah Chorus."

Hallelujah was the only word benefiting a response to the holy tale which Handel told:

> "The glory of the Lord shall be revealed"—Hallelujah!
> "Unto us a child is born"—Hallelujah!
> "The angel said unto them, Fear not"—Hallelujah!
> "Rejoice greatly, O daughter of Zion"—Hallelujah!
> "The eyes of the blind shall be opened"—Hallelujah!
> "He hath borne our griefs"—Hallelujah!
> "Worthy is the Lamb"—Hallelujah!

Yes, *hallelujah* was the right word. Ingeniously, beautifully, Handel had all of the chorus singing hallelujah together. Then, in the fourteenth line of this wonderful work, light broke again, more truth erupted with power.

Handel put it down on paper for all times, "And He shall reign for ever and ever." Suddenly, like a spark fanned into a blaze that sweeps through a field of dry grass, these words explode into the remainder of the text. Handel orchestrated it in another time and another place, but we have heard it. From the basses come the words "for ever and ever." The truth conveyed by those terms is picked up by the tenors who sing, "And He shall reign for ever." Now the words are solidly entrenched in the message and joyfully expressed in the music. Altos join the affirmation and then, almost immediately, the sopranos pick it up as well. Finally, everybody is singing "for ever." Resounding declarations of the word are bounding off each other as "for ever" is sung antiphonally again and again.

While the basses and tenors continue singing, "for ever and ever," sopranos and altos start giving voice to the regal recognition, "King of kings! and Lord of lords!" On and on that goes. But, finally, everyone comes to the same truth at the same time. So, together—with trumpets—all members of the choir sing, "And He shall reign for ever and ever, King of kings! and Lord of lords! King of kings! and Lord of lords! And He shall reign for ever and ever. Hallelujah! Hallelujah!"

Dramatically, immediately before the last hallelujah is heralded, everything stops. Silence. It is a pause, yes; a time to catch a breath, yes. But it is more. For one precious moment in time that somehow seems to transcend time, all of creation seems to come together, to rush into union, suspended in wait of an ultimate revelation. The anticipation is almost more than anyone can stand. Actually, it is only a fleeting moment, but we feel that we cannot possibly keep waiting for it to end. We are completely on edge, wanting desperately to get on with what is to be declared next, what must be said, sensing that we cannot contain a cosmic outburst of excitement for one more second. We are about to hear the definitive word of God; the final word about Advent, Christmas, God, grace, redemption, and life. It comes. Suddenly the silence is over. An explosion of joy is filled with incredible power. "Hallelujah!"

Handel saw clearly what God had done, what God is doing, and expressed it brilliantly. The "hallelujahs" and the "for evers" are all mixed up together. One depends upon the other. Each prompts the other. Handel was right. Why did I not see the truth much earlier? Never mind, thanks be to God that I see it now.

The truth of Advent and Christmas is the truth for all times. The message on the pages of this book is for all days. The baby of the manger is the Savior. He shall reign forever and ever. The Christ awaited in Advent and celebrated at Christmas is King of kings and Lord of lords forever and ever. Hallelujah. Forever! Hallelujah! Amen.

NOTES

1. Detailed instructions on how to make an Advent wreath can be found in Debbie Trafton O'Neal's *The Advent Wreath: A Light in the Darkness* (Minneapolis: Augsburg Publishing House, 1988), 13-15.

2. Instructions and suggestions for making an Advent calendar are available in Molly McConnell, *Advent: Prepare Ye the Way of the Lord* (New York: Walker and Company, 1987), 17-18; Doris Williams and Patricia Griggs, *Preparing for the Messiah: Ideas for Teaching/Celebrating Advent* (Nashville: Abingdon Press, 1987), 28-29; and Colleen Britton, "Working Advent Calendar," *Creative Ideas for Advent,* ed. Robert G. Davidson (Educational Ministries, Inc., 1980), 61-62.

3. Doris Williams and Patricia Griggs suggest twenty different decorations for a Jesse tree. Each suggestion is accompanied by notations on the person involved, biblical passages about this individual, a key Scripture text, and the appropriate symbol as well as an illustration. *Preparing for the Messiah: Ideas for Teaching/Celebrating Advent,* 31-33.

4. Alice Slaikeu Lawhead writes, "Christmas for most of us is a collection of fantastic expectations and heartbreaking disappointments." *The Christmas Survival Book* (Batavia, Ill.: Lion Publishing Corporation, 1990), 3.

5. Samples of family worship services built around an Advent wreath can be found in Dolores Walker's "Try a Family Advent Wreath," *Creative Ideas for Advent,* 21-25.

6. James E. Dittes, *Minister on the Spot* (Philadelphia: Pilgrim Press, 1970), 32-38.

7. James Weldon Johnson, *God's Trombones: Seven Negro Sermons in Verse* (New York: Penguin Books, 1978), 17.

8. G. F. Handel, *Messiah,* ed. T. Tartius Noble (New York: G. Schirmer, Inc.), 60-61.

9. Leland Wilson, *Living with Wonder* (Waco, Tx.: Word Books, 1976), 67.

10. Pam Proctor, "From the Ages, with Love: Durant on History," *Parade,* August 6, 1978.

11. Mary Ann Thomson, "O Zion Haste," *The Baptist Hymnal,* ed. Wesley L. Forbis (Nashville: Convention Press, 1991), 583.

12. Ibid.

13. Jaroslav Pelikan, *The Light of the World: A Basic Image in Early Christian Thought* (New York: Harper & Brothers, Publishers, 1962), 31.

14. John Milton, *Paradise Lost,* Book III, cited in Pelikan, *The Light of the World: A Basic Image in Early Christian Thought,* 13.

15. John S. B. Monsell, "Light of the World, We Hail Thee," *The New Church Hymnal,* ed. H. Augustine Smith (New York: Fleming H. Revell, 1937), 467.

16. Harriet Beecher Stowe, "Still, Still with Thee," *The Cokesbury Hymnal,* gen. ed. C. A. Bowen (Nashville: Abingdon-Cokesbury Press), 114.

17. Joseph E. McCabe, *Handel's Messiah: A Devotional Commentary* (Philadelphia: The Westminster Press, 1978), 37.

18. Robert Mac Gimsey, "Sweet Little Jesus Boy," Copyright 1934, Carl Fischer Inc., New York.

19. Joseph Fletcher, *Situation Ethics: The New Morality* (Philadelphia: The Westminster Press, 1966), 156.

20. McCabe, 89.

21. Richard John Neuhaus, *Freedom for Ministry* (New York: Harper & Row, Publishers, 1979), 183.

22. John Bunyan, *The Pilgrim's Progress* (New York: Books, Inc.), 9.

23. Ibid.

24. W. H. Auden, "For the Time Being: A Christmas Oratorio," *Collected Longer Poems* (Random House) cited by Ernest T. Campbell, *Locked in a Room with Open Doors* (Waco, Tx.: Word Books, Publisher, 1974), 135.

25. James S. Stewart, *King For Ever* (Nashville: Abingdon Press, 1975), 141.